Don't Mention
The Marx Brothers

— Don't Mention —
The Marx Brothers

REMINISCENCES OF S. J. PERELMAN

by Eric Lister

The Book Guild Limited
SUSSEX ENGLAND

For Irene Kemmer

The Book Guild Limited
Temple House, 25 High Street,
Lewes, Sussex
First published 1985
© Eric Lister
Set in Linotron Plantin & Helvetica
Typesetting by Central Southern Typesetters
Eastbourne 23373/21195
Printed in Great Britain by
Paradigm Print
Gateshead, Tyne and Wear

ISBN 08 6332 115 1

Contents

List of Photographs

Preface

S. J. Perelman was a great writer. He found a niche and filled it in an esoteric but immediately recognizable style. His superb phraseology blended absurdities with poetry, slang with eloquence, New York Yiddish with London Cockney and created a unique talent.

Accuracy even over the most obscure details endorsed his artistic craftsmanship, like an expert chef he knew how to blend his ingredients to perfection. Although his ambition to write a full-length novel was never fulfilled, I do believe that most of the leading novelists he admired were incapable of writing the beautifully constructed, witty, pungent short stories that he wrote so successfully.

It was not easy to make people laugh but Sydney Joseph Perelman did this through his pen for over half a century. He was frequently asked to write his autobiography but after several attempts he gave up, declaring that he could find nothing new to write about as everything he had previously written was already part of his autobiography. His works are classics of humour, and humour never dies. Sid has gone now but when you pick up one of his books and read a couple of pages at random there he is, large as life, right at your side.

Eric Lister   *London, Spring 1985*

Chapter 1

According to legend a certain distinguished gentleman by way of favour for special services rendered to the state, was invited to take tea with Her Gracious Majesty Queen Elizabeth II at Buckingham Palace.

Following this pinnacle of auspicious occasions the distinguished gentleman was discreetly questioned by a lady friend as to Her Majesty's private disposition. With barely a moment's hesitation the gentleman suavely replied, 'She was dignified, beautiful, witty, charming and intelligent'. The lady, whilst approving of her friend's glowing description of the Queen's impeccable qualities, somewhat mischievously questioned him further.

'Surely,' she asked, 'there must have been some flaw in Her Majesty's demeanour?'

To which, after some deliberation, the gentleman hesitatingly replied in hushed tones, 'Well, I suppose she was a bit of a name dropper'.

It was during a fine June afternoon in 1967, I was slouched on my rickety Thoné chair behind the flimsy desk of the minuscular Portal Gallery in London's trendy Mayfair. Opposite me seated on the only comfortable chair (out of the two we possessed at the time) was the pugnacious, funny, cynical, primitive, perceptive Mr Ringo Starr. I was so absorbed in Ringo's colourful narrative that I barely noticed the unobtrusive entrance of a slight male figure who appeared to be studying the paintings on the opposite wall of the gallery. After a few moments Ringo rose to leave. We went through our usual routine of goodbyes delivered in adenoidal Liverpudlian slang, I accompanied him to where his limousine awaited without and stepped back into the gallery to find the slight stranger still intensely scrutinizing the paintings. As I rarely look at our own paintings whilst on duty, I focused my attention on the viewee. Recognition was not instant, but my

brain eventually unclogged as I manoeuvred myself alongside him for a closer look. I observed a small ultra-dapper elderly gentleman sporting a brown Locke's★ pork-pie hat, English 'raised-seam' cheviot-tweed sports jacket, Brooks Brothers Oxford button-down shirt, silk-knitted tie, steam-pressed grey flannel trousers and hand-made well-patinated brogues.†
With some trepidation I took the plunge, 'Mr Perelman I presume'.

The face that turned towards me was a caricaturist's delight. Round and florid with jowels like antique waxed rosewood carefully shaved for half-a-century in close collaboration with Mr Gillette. The straight grey thick bristly moustache carefully matched an eyebrow (either one). Appearing beneath those bushy caterpillars were the once-seen-never-forgotten Perelman eyes. Large dark and inscrutable, the right one looking directly at me, the other staring disconcertingly over my left shoulder into infinity. The entire ocular effect was magnified by an ancient pair of minute oval silver spectacles. As memorable a trademark as the Perelman eyes was the Perelman voice. Soft, croaky, hesitant, slightly breathless and topped with an East Coast nasal twang, as American as the cherry on a chocolate malted icecream soda.

'So I am recognized in *mufti*,' was his reply. I informed him that I had seen his photograph on a book jacket.

'If it was an English publication it would have shown a postage-stamp size picture of a callow youth,' he replied. I assured him it was a recent American edition and that his visage had remained even in my defective memory.

'I trust you are not disappointed with the real thing,' he said.

The conversation then generalized about art and especially American primitives to which he admitted an addiction. After several miserable attempts on my behalf to steer the conversation around to humour, especially the Marx Brothers, I surrendered to listen to a brief account of Mr Perelman's early struggles to establish himself as an artist before turning to writing. I knew nothing of his background and was eagerly anticipating a slice, when he noticed an oil painting featuring a

---

★ *Locke's*, the celebrated English hatters, not a mispelling for American Jewish smoked salmon — a firm favourite with SJP.

† I was regrettably unable to catch sight of his socks at that moment.

superb vintage automobile in continental setting, by Neil Davenport. He asked me to tell him about the artist. I told him about the then young Davenport's jaunts across Europe with his father, a diplomatic courier, some forty years ago, and of his love of art, humour, and magnificent motor cars which he had managed to combine as a middle-aged man to produce this work.

The painting showed a young, nubile and expensively dressed female glancing knowingly at a tall handsome liveried chauffeur who was pushing a well-blanketed old man in a wheelchair towards one of those ultra-expensive art-Deco jewellery stores which abounded on the French Riviera during the late 1920s — at the kerbside stood a magnificent Hispano Suiza Landaulette.

Perelman enjoyed the description and told me of his admiration for the artist George Grosz who likewise injected humour into his work. He also told me of his own love of old cars, being the proud owner of a 1949 YT MG. His surprise at my knowledge of what a YT MG actually was, prompted him to give me a history of the car.

During one of his many rambles around the world, the first one to be precise, and accompanied by his artist friend Al Hirschfeld, he happened to be in Bangkok, Thailand, of all places, when he spotted an MG in a car showroom. Falling in love with the four-seat open touring machine he ordered one. This was to be picked up by him in London en route for his eventual triumphant return to New York.

Due to a failed link in the bureaucratic chain the little black MG was actually waiting for him at the precise time and place he had agreed! He enjoyed driving it around England for a short while before shipping it to the States in the hold of a transatlantic leviathan. The car ran like a clock from New York to Bucks County Pennsylvania where the Perelman family resided. During the next eighteen years the MG was only used for pottering around the country roads, and was cocooned in a warm barn during the winter months. During its entire 17,000 miles it had never been driven over 45 mph or exposed to bad weather. It was almost a family pet. Recently, however, age had begun to tell. Returning from an extensive two-mile tour of the local landscape one day, Mr Perelman, on stepping out of the car, could not

3

close the door as the lock and handle had fallen off somewhere en route. Despite an immediate retracing and minute scrutinization of the route on foot the missing parts were never found.

Now, several months later and after an extensive search of all the US MG agents and clubs, plus advertising in vintage car magazines, no replacement parts had been found. The immaculate car, meanwhile, was suffering the indignity of having its driver's door tied shut with pyjama cord. S. J. Perelman was therefore determined during this visit to London to find replacement parts somewhere within the British MG community. But where did one find this community? — That was his problem.

'Right up my street,' was my reply.

'Which street is that?' asked Mr Perelman.

'Not quite literally,' I replied. 'What I mean is that finding the impossible is a mission in which I revel.'

'Perhaps we can come to some arrangement,' he offered.

'Yes,' I replied, 'from now on my mission in life will be to find an MG YT driver's door lock.'

'Don't overdo it my friend,' he replied. 'Do I detect we are members of the same tribe?'

'Yes,' I replied, then, 'I'm Eric Lister.'

'I'm Sid Perelman,' we shook hands. 'As I have appointed you my official MG parts procurer we had better exchange addresses.'

I gave him a card. He took from his pocket a small crocodile-skin covered notebook and with the tiny pencil attached wrote his Pennsylvanian address. He informed me he was leaving London the next day but was a frequent visitor and perhaps we could lunch together on his next jaunt. I felt quite exalted — a hero indeed.

Humourists are few and far between, I mean *serious* humorists not *funny* people. The planet abounds with *funny* people that look identical. From London to Lhassa, Rangoon to Reykjavik, Tel Aviv to Tirana, San Francisco to Sofia; they pull the same faces, tell the same jokes, make the same crude suggestions. They appear to appease the masses and undoubtedly have done since before Mr Jesus Christ appeared, so I see no reason why they should not continue to do so when the masses reach planet Pluto.

4

To retain an element of the crude slapstick which still appeals to the masses and blend it with a literary and subtle repartée, appealing to a smaller more select section of the community requires the skill of a true humorist. Such elite twentieth century humorists as Alfred Jarry, Alphonse Allais, George and Weedon Grossmith, Robert Benchley, Jaques Tatti, Woody Allen, Mel Brooks, P. G. Wodehouse, Jerome K. Jerome, Dorothy Parker, Lennie Bruce (to name but a dozen) have tickled my fancy during the past forty years or so. Not one of these humorists had I ever met personally. It could be that half of them were dead before I could read, but they were all my heroes with their books, scripts, and records. My supreme dilemma in the 'a few of my favourite things' game would be to choose between a very sexy woman or a very funny book when I am dumped on a desert island (assuming of course that I am going to be rescued the next day). Maybe there doesn't exist such a person as a very funny and very sexy woman, but alas, up to now I have been obliged to keep my pleasures separate — some day my princess will come . . .

At the time Mr Perelman slid into my life I was definitely on a reading jag (with the odd lady assisting me with R and R). His name was adrenalin in my veins but SJP books were very hard to come by in London. His reputation amongst the general public rested on his two early Marx Brothers scripts (*Duck Soup* and *Horsefeathers*) and an early book which appeared during World War Two as a British Forces paperback edition, *Crazy like a Fox*. How British servicemen understood more than a smidgin of Perelman's esoteric mixture of Yiddish, Hollywoodeese, Eastside New York and St James's Club English, I will never know, but somehow his book attracted a small fanatical and enlightened segment who like me spent the next twenty years searching for anything new written by him. When *The New Yorker* magazine, to which I had been subscribing for many years, arrived, I frantically flicked through for the latest SJP epic, which when found, I slowly savoured. Fortunately I had been able to pick up copies of later books during my frequent visits to New York. So, when I actually met him I was reaching a Perelmanesque climax (I should be so lucky as the saying goes).

5

With my pump fully primed I searched through *Motor Sport* magazine, the British car buff's bible for MG spares and made a note of six telephone numbers in various obscure corners of England, Wales, Scotland and Ireland. I also hunted within the pages of my *Royal Automobile Club Year Book* and found the number of the MG Car Club, an organized body of which I had been a member during my sporting youth (being the sometime proud owner of an MG TC which I had raced, rallied, revved and roared through the country lanes of Merrie Olde England mostly on black market petrol).

It took me at least ten days to hit the jackpot. Most of the garages either didn't answer the 'phone (no doubt they were busily tuning twin carburettors with a stethoscope), promised to call back and in the British manner did not, or had gone out of business through being unable to pay for their advertising. The MG Car Club referred me to the MG Motor Company, which I had consulted in the first place with no success. They only stocked parts for cars from 1956 onwards. Then, amid a welter of notepads, *Motor Sports* and grubby copies of *Exchange and Mart* (Britain's buy-and-sell-everything weekly), I spotted an old MG parts specialist I hadn't tried — my last hope.

I called the Manchester number. The 'phone was eventually answered by what I mistook for an inarticulate minor bird, who told me to ''ang on'. After at least two-pounds' worth of 'anging on, a guttural Lancashire voice asked me what I wanted. I explained in detail.

He said, ''ang on,' (another two-pounds' worth!) then said, 'Yes we've got it. It's in good nick. Send me three quid and I will post it on to you.'

To my amazement he was a man of his word. Not only did the lock and handle appear within the week, but it was the correct one. I was jubilant and able to show S. J. Perelman that Eric Lister was no man of straw. Carefully packaged with customs labels reading 'One Second-Hand Car Lock and Handle, Value Three Pounds' I mailed it to 'Erwina', Bucks County.

After three weeks I received through the mail an SJP book, *Chicken Inspector No 23* inscribed:

For Eric Lister
who acted far beyond the
call of duty.

Sid Perelman

A treasure to be cherished indeed.

Chapter 2

One evening, several months later I received a telephone call at my Portobello Road flat.

'Hello, hello is that Eric Lister? This is Sid Perelman. I'm over at Brown's Hotel. If you are free for lunch tomorrow maybe we can get together.'

Modulating my eagerness I arranged to meet him around 1 pm at the gallery (just around the corner from Brown's).

Dressed as he was at our first meeting but with the addition of a Scottish tweed raglan top coat Sid arrived punctually. He seemed to be intrigued with our current exhibition which was of silk woven 'pin-ups' by Ted Wilcox — crazy colourful cloths with primitive embroideries of busty, leggy creatures such as Betty Grable, Rita Hayworth and Jane Russell, done in a manner reminiscent of the wartime *Esquire Varga* girls who had kept many a GI active under his blanket. I explained to Sid that Wilcox was an ex-RAF man who when convalescing after a wartime injury had been given embroidery as a kind of therapy. He was told to copy military insignia but after a while found it boring. So for his own and his mates' amusement he copied the *Varga* girl calendars and current poppets of the day from magazine photographs in such salubrious publications as *Tit Bits, John Bull, Silver Screen* and *Reveille* which happened to be lying around the ward. Soon Ted's 'tits 'n' arse' pics became firm favourites with the lads and after his discharge and re-entry into civvy street he continued with his 'artistic' endeavours. During the following twenty-five years or so Ted Wilcox remained a bachelor. He worked days in a West London factory and spent almost all his spare time embroidering pin-ups and contemporary news scenes, like the Queen's Coronation, Royal births, the assassination of John F. Kennedy and Jack Ruby, and often quite bizarre items that caught his fancy, but usually sprinkled with the current sex kittens. They were embroidered on cream linen dish-cloths.

A house painter friend of Wilcox was working for the British pop artist Peter Blake and mentioned Ted's 'pictures' to him. Blake was interested enough to view them and called me to say he had found a real 'pop primitive'. Soon after, my partner and I enthusiastically viewed them at Wilcox's little council house, where they entirely covered the walls; we agreed to hold an exhibition.

Sid loved them and made several notes on the back of a catalogue I had given him. Then looked up saying, 'Art always gives me a splendid appetite for *kosher* food, you wouldn't happen to know of a *haimischer* hostelry in the neighbourhood would you old boy?' I explained that Mayfair was not exactly afloat with chicken soup but in nearby Soho I knew of such an establishment called Blume's.

'Surely that's miles away in the East End, an excellent emporium,' he sighed. 'Many's the *knish* I've noshed there.'

'No,' I explained, 'that's Bloom's.'

'That's what I thought you said,' he replied.

'No.' I said. 'This is Blume's with a *U* like Blyume's.'

'Somewhat confusing,' said Sid.

'Well it is,' I admitted. 'Especially when you have two other restaurants in the vicinity both called Bloom's and rigorously denying any connection with each other of course,' I continued, 'they are obviously members of the same family who during past decades have quarrelled and gradually opened their own restaurants. But none of them has any connection with *the* Bloom's, the East End ones.'

'Well never mind the genealogical tree, what's the food like?'

'You mean at Blyume's?'

'Yes,' he croaked.

'Well, as I believe you are the connoisseur of Hebrew delicacies I will let you be the judge, let's go.'

Whilst Indian restaurants are renowned for their hideous decor, a combination of flock wallpaper, gold painted Taj Mahal style cardboard nooks and crannies, violent and clashing colours, uncomfortable seats, and dumb xenophobic waiters, English Jewish restaurants are paradoxically almost the opposite. They consist of a series of what appear to be stark hospital consulting rooms, white and decorless, inhabited by a troupe of loud-mouthed middle-aged jugglers in grubby white coats putting the customers in their place, both literally and figuratively. Usually in the vicinity of the cash till (known by the older cockney fraternity as the Jewish piano) is a begrimed framed faded photograph of an elderly bearded gentleman complete with *yarmulkah* and pears, bearing the legend — *Our Founder*.

As soon as Sid spotted the gold Mogan David on the window of Blyume's, his nose twitched and his eyes gleamed.

'The rainbow's end is nigh,' he said, as we entered the overcrowded hot and steamy establishment. Mr Blyume himself barely glanced at us as we squeezed past the glass counter where he directed operations like Captain Bligh on the bridge of the Bounty. Slicing the salt-beef* with machine gun rapidity he barked orders at the waiters with an eye constantly swivelling towards the cash till. One of the waiters pushed us into a corner table, handed us a *borscht*-stained menu and ran away. Sid glanced at the menu then at me, smiled, and said, 'Home sweet home'.

When the waiter eventually returned with a 'Well, you made up your minds yet?' Sid affixed him with the Perelman evil eye, cleared his throat and slowly ordered his favourite repast.

'I will take a bowl of *kneidlach* soup, a lean salt beef on rye, some sweet and sour cucumber and a glass of Russian tea.'

'How about a portion of home-made strudel?' hassled the waiter.

'Wait 'till I ask,' snapped Sid.

I ordered, the waiter departed. Sid turned to me and said, 'New York, London, they got the same *chutzpah*. Don't they know about English good manners?'

When the feast arrived, Sid was somewhat mollified, his food disappearing with obvious relish. After the empty plates were removed from the table, Sid carefully removed a crumb of *matzoh* from his moustache, produced a leather-bound cigarette case, tapped out a cigarette which he eventually, after several attempts with his thumb against the wheel of an immense contraption of a lighter, managed to ignite. After inhaling deeply and exhaling slowly he looked at me.

---

* US corned beef

'Uric,' he said, 'you scored another bull's-eye. It's lethal — but it's fun.'

I wondered if he meant the cholesterol-laden fare or the deadly weed or both. Being somewhat in favour of the health-food life, Jewish food, although digestable and enjoyable to me, winds up giving me emotional traumas. Not so S. J. Perelman, it appeared. Here was a man about twenty-three years older than me who had survived and thrived on it; and as I later found out he relished red meat, detested vegetables, clamoured for sweet and creamy desserts and smoked heavily. He considered food abstinence to be bunkum and although he agreed that smoking may be harmful to him he didn't consider it worth the effort to stop at his time of life. For the remainder of his visit, Blyume's was *the* spot for SJP.

The following week I arranged a little dinner at my flat for Sid to meet a few of my buddies and their respective ladies, plus, of course, my own current lady the effervescent Monique Beau, who cooked us a glorious French meal.

Sid was in great form, enjoying the company of lawyer Walter Houser, a man of similar literary and nostalgic tastes with an enviable instant-recall memory. Also present was British Member of Parliament Arthur Davidson whose sense of the ridiculous matched that of Walter's and my own and inspired Sid to reminisce on some of his more zany Hollywood experiences.

During my decade or so of close companionship with Sid, people constantly tried to manoeuvre his conversation (or sometimes lack of it) into Marx Brothers topics. This irritated him as he had been bored with the entire Marx Brothers saga for years, although he was a great admirer of their best work, especially the films he had worked on. He had not been involved with them since the mid-1930s and although, to his annoyance, he had sometimes been mistaken for Groucho (there was a distinct physical likeness) no love was lost between them. In fact often before meeting strangers he would hiss in my ear, 'Don't mention the Marx Bros.' However, occasionally when the company was mellow and he was relaxed out would pop Marx Brothers reminiscences. These were marvellous to hear first-hand but almost all of them had appeared in print over the years. My feeling was that Sid did not particularly enjoy the company of any of the Brothers outside of their professional relationship.

He did, however, befriend and respect Charlie Chaplin. He told us that around the early thirties Chaplin was in a high state of tension due to a complex variety of problems and really wanted to get away from it all for a long vacation. But where could the little man go? By that time he was famous in virtually every part of the globe and wherever he went he was besieged by 'well wishers' and admirers.

Charlie asked Sid to make some discreet enquiries through well-travelled friends as to where there might be a remote and beautiful spot where he could relax unrecognized. One of Hollywood's 'beautiful people' told Sid about the heavenly island of Bali, a virtually undiscovered paradise in the Java Sea; perfect climate, delightful artistic people, gorgeous bare-breasted ladies, dreamy music, spectacular landscapes, exciting antiquities, the lot. Sid, in turn, extolled these virtues to Chaplin putting forward the question, who could possibly know him there? Charlie was sold on the idea and soon his arrangements were made to sail for Singapore.

During the long and tedious voyage Charlie was forced to spend most of his time in his suite or be pestered continually by almost everyone on board the liner. Eventually he arrived at Singapore and as anonymously as possible transferred to a much smaller chartered vessel for his trip to the remote island paradise. Within a few days Charlie's vessel arrived at its destination and anchored about a mile offshore.

Hardly was the anchor down when a great chanting of voices was heard coming from native boats approaching their port side, as they came closer Chaplin could make out the chanting voices. Hundreds of saronged Balinese were roaring *CHARRIE! CHARRIE! CHARRIE!* Infuriated, Chaplin ducked into the cabin refusing to appear on deck and planned immediately to return as swiftly as possible to the USA.

The Captain of the vessel managed to persuade the excited natives that they should return to their island. Reluctantly they did so but after a while a particularly beautiful and sumptuous native craft appeared offside. It was being rowed by several splendidly attired Balinese males and in the covered stern sat a large elderly gentleman of obvious regal bearing. He was being fanned by lady attendants and was accompanied by two beautifully clad younger men, one of whom shouted through cupped hands to the ship's Captain. Charlie, peering through a porthole, saw all this activity and was soon informed by the Captain that the King of Bali had arrived and wished to meet him. Flattered by the Royal attention Charlie invited the King and his retinue aboard. One of the King's aides spoke some English and introduced the King to 'Charrie'. The broadly smiling King welcomed 'Charrie' to Bali. He had seen many of Chaplin's movies and was preparing a banquet in his honour at the Royal Palace to be held that very evening. An invitation that despite his trepidation Charlie could not refuse.

After a rest Chaplin, dressed in a dinner suit, was rowed ashore and met by the Royal carriage. He was taken to the ancient palace. This was much smaller and rather less grand than he had expected. Outside, under an awning he was seated formally between the King and Queen on carpet-covered rush mats before a huge banquet of unidentifiable mounds of food on platters with huge wooden bowls of rice artistically decorated by garlands of flowers and plaited grass. After many speeches, an enormous feast and an interpreted address of appreciation by Charlie, came the Gelong musicians and exquisite dancers. By now of course Chaplin was in a mellow mood and thoroughly enjoying the proceedings. Suddenly the King arose with much aid and some difficulty. He clapped his hands, the music and dancing stopped and two attendants approached carrying an enormous tray bearing a shiny, polished metal dinner service, sets of plates, dishes, pots and varied utensils. This was ceremoniously placed on a low table in front of Charlie for him to look at and admire whilst the King made a speech praising his guest of honour and gestured that he was presenting Charlie with this magnificent array of hardware. Charlie in return got to his feet to thank his host most profusely for such a magnificent gift. After which the festivities continued until dawn and a room was prepared for Charlie to sleep off the effects.

Later in the day when Charlie had awoken and the tender had arrived to take him back to the boat, he found the dinner service carefully packed in leaves and straw, ready to be transported by native canoe to his boat. Just as he was about to make his friendly departure one of the King's attendants smilingly approached him.

'Preeze, Mr Charrie now pay for prates,' he said indicating the packed set awaiting. Chaplin was unable to believe his ears.

'You mean I am supposed to pay for this?' he asked, indicating the 'gift'.

Bowing and beaming, the aide haltingly explained that 'Charrie' had agreed to, but at a special discount price (the equivalent of one thousand US dollars) which was at least half the regular price because the King loved 'Charrie' so much. At that Chaplin beat a hasty retreat in anger, followed by a gaggle of Royal attendants imploring him to pay and stay. The somewhat crestfallen King hovered in the background limply waving to the steamer which was already setting sail in the general direction of Beverly Hills.

Chapter 3

Sid adored observing the British aristocracy especially in their native habitat. The upper crust was his 'glass of tea' as he remarked. Once the word got around the Debrett's and Burke's set that this was the man that wrote for the Marx Brothers, despite the fact that it was over thirty years previously, S. J. Perelman was 'in'.

The odd Black person, pop musician, TV personality or New York Jewish writer was acceptable and on certain occasions even desirable. Sid and I once appeared together in a photograph which graced the society pages of one of the uniquely British glossy magazines. This was the accolade of acceptance. A springboard for Sid to enjoy himself amongst the hoipolloi. He received invitations from Lords and Ladies, Sirs and Right Honourables to spend the weekend 'In the contray'. Sid rarely refused an invitation where good food and wine flowed freely. His little crocodile-skin address book was filled with illustrious monikers. He began to take on a somewhat Wodehousian air.

Anybody who is anybody living in Mayfair, Knightsbridge or Belgravia spends the weekend 'in the contray'. He suggested that those that did not keep their window blinds down and cars parked around the corner to prevent any of their acquaintances who found it generally necessary to remain occasionally in town noticing their presence.

Sid was soon befriended from Wiltshire to Westmoreland, where he told a few amusing stories no doubt, but spent most of his time listening and later writing hilarious accounts of it all. On one such occasion he recalled that Princess Margaret (whom he described as quite a dish) was having difficulty with a non-functioning gold cigarette lighter.

Sid observed this and with the agility of a gazelle (before any of the several other nearby males had time to budge) leapt to her aid with his ancient trusty contraption at the ready and already blowing a jet like an oil-well fire. The Royal coiffure was no doubt saved from singing only because of the length of HRH's cigarette holder. Princess Margaret thanked Sid and engaged him in conversation about the unreliability of her cigarette lighter. Sid still standing like the Statue of Liberty with flaming torch in his left hand snapped his lighter closed with a great clunk. Her Royal Highness was intrigued with the strange contraption. Sid explained that it was made exclusively for him by a small pipemaker in New York and once you got the knack of thumbing the wheel it never failed. I'm sure he didn't tell her that he didn't always have the knack. However Sid's offer of the lighter was graciously accepted as a gift. If I ever meet Princess Margaret I will pay particular attention to the condition of the top of her right thumb.

This incident promoted one of Sid's best unwittingly throw-away lines. The next day he asked me for a light for his cigarette, 'Where's your blow torch?' I asked.

'Oh,' was his nonchalant reply, 'I gave it to Princess Margaret.'

Sid rarely mixed his friends, only his metaphors. Therefore his stories of hilarious jaunts to this or that English stately home, moulding Scottish ruin or Irish eccentric's retreat were usually recounted over a steaming bowl of Barbara's chicken soup, with an audience of Max and I spluttering *matzoh* crumbs over the tablecloth. American writer Max Wilk and his artist wife Barbara lived during this period in the Belsize Park area of North London. It was either to the Wilks or I that Sid let his hair down and 'tried out' his accounts of recent escapades.

During the winter months Sunday brunch at the Wilks' house became almost a ritual, assuming of course, Sid was 'available'. Often those winter afternoons developed into a kind of humorists' jam session where London's remaining Hollywood ex-patriots and old cronies of SJP and the Wilks would drop in for a *schmooze*. Each one triggering off some long-forgotten episode about the high jinks and scandal in the celluloid city. The 'gig' was occasionally attended by neighbour Dr Slattery and the actor Peter O'Toole, both adding an Irish flavour to the proceedings. These intimate gatherings were Sid's greatest pleasure. He needed the

16

company of the Wilks, the Shensons, the Getz, Maurice Binder and all his *haimischer* friends. The blue bloods tickled his palate but it was the chicken soupers that provided him with the nourishment. I guess he thought that kedgeree and *kreplach* didn't mix.

On his visits to London Sid was occasionally accompanied by his wife Laura. They had been married almost forty years. There was a son, Adam and a daughter, Abbey, who were by that time leading their own lives. Around 1969, Sid and Laura rented a mews flat in Mayfair. Unfortunately they did not stay there for long as Laura became sick and preferred to return to Bucks County. Sadly, shortly afterwards, Laura's illness proved to be terminal. It was after the shock of his wife's death that Sid decided to leave the USA permanently and sell the estate before settling in London. During the intermediate period Sid resided at a New York hotel, the Gramercy Park where he continued writing for his old favourites *The New Yorker* and *Travel and Leisure* magazine amongst others.

One particularly amusing piece he wrote for *The New Yorker* just prior to Laura's passing was based on the embroidery art of Ted Wilcox which, of course, he had seen a few months back at Portal Gallery. He 'wove' an hilarious tale about purchasing this piece of naïve tea-towel art for his wife's wedding anniversary gift. The sarcastic remarks of the Kennedy Airport customs officer when Sid declared it was a work of art and his wife's thinly veiled disdain; she thought it was a one-dollar-fifty tea-towel. Her eventual compromise by displaying it in the guest bathroom and Sid's nagging concern for its welfare in the steam-laden atmosphere (so much so that he eventually gave it a coat of shellac as a kind of preservative). The total disaster of Mrs Reifsnyder the cleaning lady sending it to the laundry to remove its coating of grease and Sid's crazy chase to the laundry and eventually (his favourite story location) a seedy Philadelphian cleaning establishment run by a Mr Turtletaub. This sleazy individual was at odds to understand Sid's concern over a cheap tea-towel he described as Atlantic City *schlock*. When it was eventually produced, shrunk to the size of a pocket handkerchief with all the artwork distorted, Sid nearly had a seizure, bleating wildly about his lawyers suing, 'A work of art destroyed,' and other such outbursts. Eventually, calmed down by the sight of Turtletaub's partner carrying a pipe-wrench, Sid settled for an apology and offer to mothproof his sweater free of charge, putting the entire episode down to his own inexperience in purchasing naïve art.

'Next time,' he said, 'I'll make sure it is sanforized.'

Chapter 4

Early in the 1970s S. J. Perelman gathered together his
portmanteau, crates of books, records and lifetime's
paraphernalia, booked a transatlantic sea passage and set sail
for merry England. He was fortunate finding amiable
company like Ludovic Kennedy aboard. In good spirits and
ever on the look-out for a seaboard romance, particularly of
the young Wilcox-blonde-leggy kind, Sid had a ball.

I was alerted by telegram to meet him dockside. He duly
appeared, brown pork-pie at a jaunty angle, clutching his
constant companion the small early portable typewriter he
invariably worked on. He was directing a steward pushing a
trolley-load of battered leather luggage. Each case smothered
in tattered labels from obscure hotels like The Imperial
Rangoon or mercifully forgotten defunct Lebanese shipping
lines. Hovering in the background was a spotty faced youth
holding a hand-written card bearing the name 'Mr Perelman'.
After our brief back-slapping session and Sid's 'Good to see
you old boy,' I piloted an obviously irate SJP in the direction
of the youth. With a penetrating glance Sid fired a high-
pitched verbal fusillade towards him.

'You are no doubt from G— and Company,' (the shipping
agents). The youth gulped and nodded in acknowledgment.

'Well, I am S. J. Perelman and I was highly recommended
to your company; already I find your New York colleagues
have mislaid two of my valuable crates *and* I am now informed
by my steward that one of three crates being unloaded has split
open. God knows what damage has been done, I must speak
with your supervisor, immediately.'

The youth mumbled something about inspecting the
damage and 'phoning the office.

'Where is the office?' cried Sid.

'Well Sir, it is a nearby building about three minutes' walk.'

'OK let's go.'

I pointed out that the steward was waiting to unload his

trolley and that my car was parked nearby. So, in procession the four of us (the youth still bearing the 'Mr Perelman' card trailing in the rear) went to my car. After a great deal of hassle we managed to load the little car with so much stuff that it began to look like an Irish tinker's caravan. During the proceedings in which he commandeered the services of the somewhat unwilling youth Sid obviously grew more and more irritable as I became more and more concerned with the groaning suspension on my car. Eventually the car was fully stuffed and the steward stood around obviously waiting for his (hopefully generous) tip. Sid told me he had nothing but traveller's cheques and could I lend him a few quid 'till we got to London. This currency he brandished in the face of the steward informing him that as the car was now full of valuable possessions he would be required to stand guard until our return from the shipping office.

Turning to me he snapped, 'Uric, I would prefer you to come with us'.*

So off we marched leaving a distinctly disgruntled steward. Sid was somewhat mollified in the office when he was informed the missing boxes had been found in New York, would be flown over and delivered to London at the company's expense during the next few days and that the split case was already outside for him to inspect.

This little ceremony was duly performed by Sid accompanied by the over-weight, perspiring agent. No serious damage was found and it was agreed that the crate should be roped and dispatched to London the next day. We returned to the car, the surly steward was duly rewarded and we drove off towards London. This was the first time I had witnessed Sid's grumpy side emerge on the surface. He bristled and his pallor visibly purpled when confronted by inefficient lackeys (and no doubt *latkes*). Funnily enough I revelled in his smouldering temper. So long as I was not the object of his anger. He reminded me of me. A curmudgeon from way back, and there are not too many of us around.

On our drive to London, despite the decidedly cramped

---

*One of SJP's self-imposed regulations was, if the issue is in doubt take a witness with you.

conditions and his periodic admonishments to me to slow down, his temper abated and his enthusiasm for the imagined delights of London life emerged. He had rented a large and comfortable Victorian flat in a fashionable Kensington Square.

'One of the reasons I specified this location,' he confided, 'was because of its close proximity to your own flat. Why waste *gelt* on taxis, old boy?'

I enquired how he had discovered such a sumptuous accommodation.

'Oh a well-connected dame I happen to know used her influence with an estate company and . . . bingo.'

'Have you actually seen it yet?' I asked.

'Well, no,' he admitted. 'But this dame has got terrific taste and what suits her suits me.'

'Sid, you mean great taste or great knockers?' I asked.

'Why it's not possible for both?' he queried.

Although the mysterious lady never appeared before me in person if her knockers were as good as her taste she must have been a peach, because the apartment was in excellent taste. Sid was delighted and euphoria reigned for forty-eight hours. All the stuff arrived as promised and he executed a *kazatzka* amongst his crates and portmanteau. Gradually the euphoria tarnished as Sid realized how difficult it was to get anything done in London.

Firstly, he would call me to pop over and fix his toaster before we ate dinner at a local bistro. He explained that he had changed the plug, switched on, put the bread in and ten minutes later taken the bread out, to discover it was exactly the same colour and temperature as when it went in.

'Where's your voltage transformer?' I asked.

He looked bemused, 'What's that?' he asked.

'In the US you run on 110 volts, or thereabouts, over here it's around 240 volts so none of your electrical equipment will work without transformers.'

'Shit, what can I do?' he croaked.

'Get transformers,' I replied. 'Try the South Kensington electrical stores for starters, but right now let's go eat.'

I introduced him to South Ken's mecca for past-their-prime Polish expatriates. A relic of the 1940s where one could still get a bowl of steaming home-made *borscht*, a slice of rye bread,

21

Polish sausage, sauerkraut and a cream cake for a pittance. Sid gnawed his way through the lot with obvious delight, at the same time appreciating the surrounding diners. Most definitely 'The 1935 Cracow Set'.

Ladies carefully attired in outrageous hats and furs, gentlemen immaculately suited. The assembly engaged in a babble of Polish conversation, whilst puffing away through cigarette holders, sipping lemon tea and carefully balancing exotic pastries on pronged forks. Occasionally a new arrival would be welcomed with a little bow and a hearty handshake. As most of the formally attired elderly Polish male patrons appear to average about five foot two in height and the hat rack is mounted about six foot above the basement stairs one of our favourite pastimes was watching these old codgers on tip-toe attempting to chuck their homburgs on to a peg. Sometimes, when a hat rolled down the stairs Sid and I almost rolled off our chairs trying to stifle our chuckles. Nobody else in the place ever seemed to notice this or the fact that the window seat was almost entirely occupied by two enormous mangy cats which appeared to be pets of the two old dames who sat wreathed in smoke behind the cash desk. It was all great copy for Sid, and as he enjoyed the excellent food, low price and good service. The 'Polish place' soon became his local café.

For a change of atmosphere or a romantic tryst with one of his *femmes fatâle* he dined at an excellent Thai restaurant in the locality. It has always been socially acceptable to eat at an inexpensive restaurant if it is oriental. Also, as Sid mentioned, hot food 'turned 'em on' and it was only five minutes walk from his king-sized bed.

The fixing of the flat became a mixture of tedium and hilarity. Sid's prowess as a DIY man was not as developed as his command of English, so he would check in at the gallery during the day and after calling a series of plumbers, electricians, decorators and window cleaners who promised but invariably failed to call back, we would go to his place armed with Woolworth's best paint, fuse wire, plugs, washers etc. My own skill as an oddjob man was legendary throughout Albania during the reign of King Zog but I was a little out of practice that year. Our combined efforts to repair broken lamps and unblock sinks were invariably doomed to failure.

So Sid remained at the mercy of the British workman. It was difficult to convince him that the average British workman of the 1970s was totally opposite to his counterpart of the 1930s. Sid's exasperation simmered and boiled to the danger level. The respectable, capable and skilful craftsman in his memory's eye invariably (when they occasionally did keep an appointment) turned out to be a beer-bellied, tattooed yob who bodged and charged excessively. S. J. Perelman was not a man to be trifled with especially by menials. I was expecting an explosion of Krakatoan proportions any day. So when a buddy of mine recommended Mr Withers an oddjob man of advanced years who was decidedly of the old school I made the connections and took him to meet Sid.

A faint gleam in Sid's offside eye signalled to me that he approved of Mr Withers. In the classic *Upstairs-Downstairs* tradition Mr Withers retired to the hall whilst Sid discussed his potential qualifications with me. All I could repeat was that the old gentleman had been highly recommended to me by a reliable friend. Mr Withers was duly engaged on a month's trial as a kind of oddjob man cum retainer. He was put on a weekly wage for several hours work daily and worked out well. He and Sid came to a swift understanding and developed a mutual respect. Gradually, the odd jobs were completed, the bathroom painted and the windows cleaned. They even ate fish and chip lunches together on the kitchen table and made side trips to the launderette; the definitive odd couple.

When Sid appeared at the gallery around lunchtime we would usually mooch over to the Nuthouse, a Soho vegetarian restaurant, owned by myself and partner. Although I am not a vegetarian I do enjoy health food which was anathema to Sid. As we crossed Regent Street I began to feel the force of a mental tug of war developing between us as Sid started to stride purposefully towards Blyume's, I toward Nuthouse. I gave in to him on several occasions but never he to me. The closest we got to compromise was Sid seated in the Nuthouse. On the table in front of him a large untouched salad, on a chair beside him, covered by a napkin was a Blyume's salt-beef on rye sandwich from which he periodically grabbed a bite as inconspicuously as possible. This exercise gave him great joy, especially the fact that (adding insult to injury), I, the boss, had personally smuggled it into the Nuthouse.

In the heart of Mayfair there is an extremely posh florist's establishment patronized by anyone who is anyone including you know who. Sid spent hours padding around Mayfair and St James seeking out ancient emporiums, hatters, shirtmakers, sports-clothes shops (especially the type that featured a *veltschoen* shoe in a slimy tank of water), taxidermists, tobacconists and gentleman's hairdressers patronized by Prince Frederick of Lower Slabovia. Not to mention specialist book stores and cheese shops. He had not previously expressed an interest in horticulture so I was intrigued when he asked me to accompany him to view some plants. We entered the posh florist. Sid was effusively greeted by a gentlewoman wearing a green smock.

'Oh, you are the American gentleman who was in yesterday,' she squeaked. Sid, delighted to be recognized, spoke of the two plants he had looked at yesterday.

'Of course sir, you mean the *Crassula succulentes*, please follow me.'

She led us into an inner jungle and smilingly pointed to two huge potted plants the heavy trunks and limbs of which were encrusted with small damp bright green leaves.

'Aren't they beauties Sir?' she said. 'At least twenty years old.'

Sid enquired about their origin and was told they came from Africa, where in some parts they were known as elephant plants because of the elephant's partiality for succulent leaves. An astronomical price was mentioned which Sid appeared to consider within reason as he suggested to me that we purchase one each. On an impulse I agreed and the next day they were delivered to our respective apartments. Mine was seated on an oak Cromwellian table by the window where it resides to this present day. Sid could not find a suitable spot so placed his on a rickety side table by the door. Clearly the 'Crassula' was none too happy in this spot because after a few weeks Sid complained to me that his plant was looking distinctly droopy, whilst mine was particularly perky. He suggested we return to the Mayfair 'Gardens of Babylon' for specialist advice. The elderly lady assistant once again recognized Sid, and with a high-pitched squeak said, 'Oh, Mr Perelman how nice to see you again, how are the plants?'

'Well,' said Sid, 'Mr Lister's plant is thriving, mine seems to be drooping.'

'Oh, I am so sorry,' cooed the lady. 'Has it got enough light? Are you adhering to the watering instructions? Not too much you know. Plants require care,' she remonstrated.

Sid somewhat shamefacedly admitted that the plant resided in the gloomier and draughtier area of the living room and that he would move it into the full daylight at the earliest possible moment. This meant that Mr Withers, directed by Sid, had to *schlep* it on the rickety table to a spot alongside the sofa which in turn resided by the window. Despite its improved location the plant continued to deteriorate. A constant buffeting each time Sid walked past did not improve the situation. Then one evening I had a call from Sid telling me that the plant was shedding leaves fast and on close examination he had found red spots appearing on the branches. He was worried and did I think he should contact the florist?

Promptly at 9 am Sid telephoned the shop and was told he must bring the plant in for an immediate examination. Not a man who usually used taxis freely he considered this to be an emergency and within half-an-hour was collecting me in a plant-filled taxi. The old dear was waiting with a porter and trolley, the plant was bundled into a back entrance as quickly and inconspicuously as possible. We entered the emporium where the old lady and a sombre gentleman introduced as the manager were examining the plant through a large magnifying glass. After a few anxious moments and a whispered discussion between them the lady spoke quietly to Sid.

'Mr Perelman, I fear your plant may be suffering from the Red Mealy disease.'

Sid looked positively shocked, 'Are you sure?' he asked.

'Well, not certain,' she admitted, 'but we think so.'

'Is it terminal?' Sid asked.

'Not necessarily so,' said the assistant. 'But it will need drastic treatment to save it, and we will have to act without delay.' Sid hesitated before commenting, as she went on, 'We will treat the plant with a special solution, remove all affected parts and repot it. Then it will be up to you to give it as much tender loving care as possible'.

Sid turned towards me at this point and I thought I noticed his inscrutable expression give way to a barely perceptible wink. With a little throat clearing he addressed the florists present.

'Do you think we could take a second opinion before embarking on such a drastic solution?' he asked. 'You see, by pure coincidence a dear friend of mine is right here in London at the moment attending a conference, he is Professor Jellinek of the Peoples' Horticultural Institute of Budapest and I feel confident I could persuade him to add his diagnosis.'

The manager appeared rather taken aback at Sid's idea but solemnly agreed to the suggestion. En route from the emporium to the gallery Sid mirthfully outlined his scheme.

'How about playing along with these people and asking Lionel Levy [my partner] to act the part of the good professor?'

'Love to,' I replied.

Over a Blyume's chopped liver sandwich, a somewhat reluctant Lionel was persuaded to accompany us back to the shop. His condition was that he didn't understand English and he and Sid were to converse to the absolute minimum in Slavic-sounding syllables (which actually turned out to be pidgin Yiddish).

We were ushered into the back room by the old dear, the manager joined us and Sid introduced them to 'Professor Jellinek' who responded with a little bow. The 'Crassula' was carefully inspected through a glass by Lionel, he and Sid then had a short unintelligible discussion. A poker-faced Sid explained to the anxious lady and manager that the Professor did not speak English very well but he wished them to know that their diagnosis was correct, it was the dreaded Red Mealies. Also, that he considered their remedy the only solution.

The manager arranged to treat the plant accordingly, promised to send Mr Perelman a weekly report on its progress and gave him a pot of geraniums with the compliments of the establishment. A rather embarrassed Lionel was complimented on his performance by Sid as we strolled through Mayfair enjoying our jolly jape. It was touch and go for the next two weeks but I am pleased to report that a considerably slimmed but fit-looking plant was delivered back to Sid after a month. It was reallocated to its position on the rickety table by the sofa where it continued to get under Sid's feet and put him into a state of nervous caution through fear of

26

knocking it over.

To my surprise, several weeks later an unshaven Sid arrived at my flat early one morning.

'Uric,* how about a cup of coffee?' he asked. 'I've just had a night of loath when I should have had a night of love.' I suggested that he simmer down and explain himself.

'It's that fucking plant — it's driving me *meshugge*,' he snarled.

'How?' I asked.

'How! I'll tell you how! You will recall me describing to you that divine long-stemmed popsy I met at the Culver-Brown's weekend party, well, a couple of weeks back I met her purely by chance outside the launderette on Bute Street. She greeted me affectionately and we spent a pleasant hour dissecting cream cakes and getting better acquainted in the nearby coffee house. Last week we went to a theatre and dined afterwards during which time I could feel my passion arousing when she frequently made gestures and dropped hints as to the intimate pleasures we would be enjoying in the near future.' He paused to light a cigarette, inhaled and sipped more fresh coffee.

'Last night I arranged for a Chinese take-away dinner to be delivered to my place. The gorgeous creature arrived dressed in a most alluring gown displaying her delicious boobs to full advantage. We managed to display a certain amount of physical restraint whilst picking through the Chinese delicacies and she polished off three glasses of cold Chablis.'

He gave a dry cough, drank more coffee and carried on with his tale of woe. 'It was obvious to me that she was as hot for me as I was for her and it was the right moment to put my plan into operation. I took her hand, led her to the sofa where the preliminaries commenced, as she loosened her bodice, I removed my tie. We snuggled close.'

He breathed heavily and paused for a minute. 'As our lips met, my hand slid gently between her cleavage, she pulled away slightly and murmured into my ear, "Sid be a darling and turn the lights down". Hardly knowing what I was doing I arose from the sofa. There was a tremendous crash as I knocked over the plant complete with the table. One badly busted plant lay in a pile of soil and leaves next to the

---

*Pronounced Eric by most people but "Uric" by SJP.

upturned table. I froze in horror, my passion quickly abating to be replaced by anger. Turning to look at my night's great expectation I saw her already buttoning her dress and about to put her shoes on. "Sid," she admonished, "how could you be so clumsy? Look what you have done to that lovely plant, and all that mess on your beautiful carpet. I think I'd better go home now I feel sick. It must have been the wine." "Look," I pleaded with her, "I can clean this mess up with the hoover in no time and then we could . . ." She interrupted, "Maybe another time Sid, now can you 'phone for a taxi?"

'In ten minutes she was gone and I was on my knees furiously cleaning up the mess.'

He paused again for another cigarette. 'Of course,' he went on, 'I didn't sleep a wink and when Mr Withers arrived this morning I dispatched him pronto to the garden centre to hire a wheelbarrow.'

'What for?' I queried.

'To bring the plant around to you. I am making you a present of it. It will be arriving any moment.'

'But Sid . . .' I started, only to be interrupted by the arrival of Mr Withers pushing a bloody great barrow-load of soil and plant. It took us a couple of hours to repot, reprune and generally tidy the now much smaller specimen. I placed it in a choice window spot where it resides healthily to this day now as large as its twin, I guess they missed each other.

Chapter 5

About twenty years before I met Sid he had been involved with the spectacular Hollywood showman Avram Goldbogen, more familiarly known to the general public as Mike Todd. Sid loved to recount hilarious stories of Todd's hyper-extravagances and shady deals. He had been approached by him to join a group of writers working on the screenplay of Jules Verne's epic, *Around the World in Eighty Days*. This was really Sid's dish of tea. He had admired Verne's works since childhood. Their meticulous detail and vivid imagination fascinated him and after all, Jules Vernes was the original 'travel writer'. So he plunged into the assignment with gusto.

Like most of his Hollywood counterparts Todd was more concerned with speed and cost than accuracy. He had engaged an enormous cast of superstars headed by David Niven who was to play the all-British hero Phileas Fogg. The size of the production was mind-boggling. All Todd had to do was find the money and make the deals. After several hectic months working with Todd in Hollywood Sid's scenario was completed. The writing was easy he said, it was extracting his money from Todd that was the tough part. It got so bad that Sid would not part with a page of script until Todd paid him cash on the nail. They usually met in a car lot where Sid would swap a couple of pages for a fistful of dollars; this developed into a regular routine. Todd would be waiting, reclining in the back of an enormous Cadillac, puffing on a ten-inch Havana; Sid would arrive in a cab. Todd's chauffeur opened a rear door; Sid got in. The deal was consummated; the whole scene was repeated a couple of nights later. Towards the end of the colossal production even the stars were working on a cash-and-carry basis.

At one point during the production Todd was in a mighty dilemma over a scene which was supposed to take place in nineteenth century Bangkok. He was planning to build a replica fleet of the Royal Siamese barges and employ hundreds of extras in full regalia to row them. This of course, involved the whole caboodle being transported to a river in California which in turn would have mock Siamese period buildings constructed on the bank. Another enormous expense which Todd in his near bankrupt condition could not find. A frivolous suggestion by Sid saved the day. He had been a pal of Benny Goodman for years and remembered that the King of Thailand was a great admirer of the King of Swing. He adored jazz, attempted to be a clarinet player and owned all of Benny's records. Now, if the King could be approached with the 'I am a friend of Benny Goodman' routine he might be persuaded to put on a Royal Barge display, the genuine article. In turn, this would only require a small film crew to fly to Thailand at a minimal cost compared with the alternative. The great showman took Sid seriously and with admirable *chutzspah* contacted the Thai King. His Majesty thanked Todd for the enormous box of jazz records received by air. He thought that the publicity involved would give a great boost to Thailand's tourist trade and agreed to put on a Royal Barge show for the movie.

When Sid was clearing out a barnload of books before leaving Bucks County he came across the gilt-edged, buckram-bound copy of *Around the World in Eighty Days* which Todd had sent him before he was hired. He decided to re-read it, and became fired with a new idea.

It was now some twenty-five years since the movie, which after all, was only a parody of Verne's original masterpiece. Why couldn't he re-do the trip, sticking as closely as possible to the story. Verne's love of detail was a challenge to Sid. Maybe when he moved to London he could investigate the possibility.

On several occasions Sid talked to me about the idea. After all, he reasoned, he too, like the fictional Phileas Fogg was a member of the Reform Club. One day he even went to the extent of counting his strides from the Savile Row Fogg residence to the Reform. Not exactly the number specified by Verne in his novel, but near enough. This puzzled Sid as he knew that Verne hadn't even visited London, never mind travel around the world. Apart from a few continental forays Verne had remained in France throughout his entire life. So how the heck did he know the distance from Savile Row to the

Reform Club in Pall Mall? He must have been one helluva researcher. Sid's intrigue with the mixture of facts and fiction woven by Verne was tempered by the fact that it was now one century later and people used slightly different modes of transport. It would be no *yiches* to makes a trip around the world in eighty days, eighty hours maybe.

He had done the immediate post-World-War-Two trip with Al Hirschfeld out of which emerged the very funny book *Eastward Ha*. Now his publishers, *The New Yorker*, and other papers and magazines were very interested in the new project so certain finance would be readily available.

Back in the States he met an ideal female companion for the trip, his own version of Fogg's faithful servant Passepartoute, maybe not as versatile or efficient but certainly better to look at. She met Sid's visual requirements to a tee and she was a bright lady as I later found out when I met her in London. Sid invented one of his delicious names for her, Sally Lou Claypool, a siren from the Deep South. She was in fact Diane Baker. Sid's preparation and kitting out for the trip kept him busy for weeks. He enjoyed his forays with bespoke tailors and shoemakers. His encounters with British travel agents who spent hours with him ploughing through obscure shipping line schedules, finding steam train connections in Turkey and booking in at hotels in Alahabad or Penang. This was the old SJP and begone dull care.

Finally departure day arrived. I met with a small group of his closest friends and journalists at the Reform Club for a champagne send-off. He looked frail and vulnerable as he stepped into the horse-drawn handsome cab, followed by the gorgeous 'Passepartoute'. The photographers' flashbulbs lit the winter gloom as the cab clip-clopped off to Victoria Station, in much the same manner as Fogg had done a century earlier. We all followed in cars and taxis to the station. On the platform I handed him a parcel of his favourite Bendick's Sporting & Military chocolate. He clutched his Gladstone bag; Diane posed for more cheesecake pics by the train compartment door. Soon, with a cheer from all of us, they were off. I knew S. J. Perelman was considerably tougher than he looked.

During his many adventures and misadventures en route, which he later wrote about in *Around the Bend in Eighty Days*, he kept me up to date with his progress by sending postcards from obscure places. One such Turkish armpit of iniquity was Erzurum, a place I had known and told him about. The postcard confirmed and magnified my own impressions. He concocted a lovely title for his chapter about this episode in 'Around the Bend'. To get to his destination from Istanbul he took the night train, hence, *When The Midnight Choo Choo Leaves for Erzurum*.

As I had a copy of his schedule I figured the approximate date he would reach Singapore. So, one lunchtime I went into Blyumes, where the patron was still slicing the salt-beef. When I finally caught his attention I asked him for a spare menu to send to a friend of mine. This request he couldn't figure out and whilst still slicing and till-watching he said, 'Why you need a menu if he ain't here?'

'It's for S. J. Perelman,' I replied.

'Who?'

'You know,' I replied, 'the American man that's been coming here three times a week for the past six months.' No sign of recognition from Blyume. I continued, 'The famous Jewish writer, well he has gone on a trip around the world in eighty days and I want to send him a menu from his favourite restaurant.'

Blyume continued slicing as he replied, 'Some customer, he goes away for eighty days'.

I got the menu, wrote on it Sid's address which was Raffles Hotel, Singapore and mailed it to him. He later assured me it brought tears to his eyes. The last section of his trip was completed without 'Sally Lou Claypool' who for mysterious personal reasons returned to the land of cotton, leaving Sid on his Tod.* (I couldn't help it.)

He became Passepartouteless in jolly old Honkers† where fortunately his many friends and press club buddies wined and dined him to the brink. From the British colony he headed for Tokyo, San Francisco and New York. Returning to England aboard the last of the Atlantic leviathans Queen Elizabeth II. His return to London was anticlimactic, his feelings and emotions about the trip none too happy. He was just glad to be

* In cockney rhyming slang, Tod is short for Tod Malone, alone. Geddit?
† Hong Kong

back in his South Ken pad.

After the statutory eighty days had passed Sid rather mischieviously paid a visit to the Reform Club. He approached the venerable desk-porter (who eighty days previously had wished him God speed on his journey), to collect his mail.

The elderly retainer peered enquiringly, 'What name Sir?'

Chapter 6

The social scene and his buddies welcomed Sid back, he was inundated with invitations to recount his adventures over dinner which was one of Sid's favourite pastimes. Another was accompanying me to the jazz clubs and bars where I played clarinet and sang blues around London. Sid was a jazz person, not only did he 'dig' the sounds of his favourites, Duke Ellington, Benny Goodman, Jess Stacey, Errol Garner, but he loved the jazz jargon and the musicians' special brand of humour. Most of the jazz fraternity knew all about S. J. Perelman and when I introduced him to fellow musos he was in great demand. Often he would look in at the Troubadour coffee house in Earls Court, where I did a regular Friday night gig with my four-piece swing band.

We usually wound up in Mike and Sheila Van Bloemen's apartment above the club where Sid would sit drinking coffee with a bunch of jazz people, telling stories of the early days of jazz in New York and his favourite times. The era when Benny was just becoming King of Swing. When Goodman appeared in London he took me to a concert at the Albert Hall. Backstage Sid gave his name and we were immediately ushered into Benny Goodman's dressing room. I had heard stories about Benny being another member of the curmudgeon club but with me he was a charming and interesting man. We were his guests to dinner at a trendy Chelsea restaurant. After the meal he came over and chatted with me about the British jazz scene and asked my opinion of his British band.

'Sid tells me you are a clarinet player,' he said.

'Well I've been trying for years,' I admitted.

Goodman was a boyhood hero of mine and here he was asking me for my musical opinions. I felt like Father O'Brian being asked for advice by the Pope (well, maybe Reb Pletz and the Chief Rabbi).

Sunday mornings we alternated between Merlin's Cave, a North London jazz club in a pub which Sid liked, or my own place Waldo's Winery on Edgware Road. I got in (a little too early) on the seventies wine bar craze and enjoyed a limited success. We had an open house jam session, 12 to 2 pm Sundays, anybody could blow in and frequently did. Sid would drink a glass of wine, swallow a sausage and ask us to play *Apple Honey* or *Stomping at the Savoy*.

Another of Sid's friends I enjoyed meeting was Alistair Cooke. As a 'radio fanatic' school kid listening to Benny Goodman's latest records played on the BBC *Jazz Club* I was also familiar with Alistair Cooke's *Letter from America*. Cooke, of course was better known in this country than America until relatively recently when he became a TV star with his excellent *America* series. Here in Britain millions have recognized his mid-Atlantic accent for several decades. He originated from Blackpool the north of England's Atlantic City, and the scene of many childhood escapades for me. We resided in nearby Manchester and dad took us to Blackpool several times each summer. The first one of us to spot the spectacular Blackpool Tower from the back seat of his Chrysler would get a silver threepenny bit.

One very snowy evening Sid and I were invited to the Cooke's temporary London house for drinks. Alistair was as suave, witty and interesting as I had expected and, of course, he was another jazz person. Midway through Jane Cooke's yummy canapés we were plunged into darkness (*plunge* according to the *Little Oxford Dictionary* means 'immerse completely'). Well, as we were not participating in an Agatha Christie 'whodunnit', we suspected an electrical failure. Through the usual 'ohs' and 'ahs' I heard Sid cursing his cigarette lighter as it failed to ignite. Finally the dragon came to life and breathed fire thereby illuminating the room. The Cooke's and Sid's first reaction was to call an emergency electrician, I suggested to them that they were not in USA and here emergency usually meant within twenty-four hours. Jane found some candles in the kitchen. Holding one of them aloft we all trooped monk-like down in to the cellar where I found and repaired a fuse. Not exactly an act of high technology but I was applauded and assured by the group that without me they would still have been in darkness. Knowing of Sid's prowess as an electrician I added 'Permanently'.

As the Cooke's were due at some nearby venue for dinner pretty soon they began 'phoning taxis and mini cabs, without any success. Everything halts for two inches of snow in London. So 'Our Hero' suggested that if they would care to squeeze into a Porsche I would be happy to drive them. We squeezed Sid into the rear, knocking his hat off in the process. He was too compressed to complain, he just groaned. Alistair and Jane crushed in alongside me, I started the engine depressed the clutch and painfully manoeuvred my arm in search of the gear lever. I thought I had found it when there was a chilly remonstration from Jane.

'What on earth do you think you are up to?' she asked.

Horrified I snatched my hand from between her knees and choked out a profuse and very sincere apology, grabbed the gear shift and drove off through the snow. One day someone will ask me what was my most embarrassing moment; I will have instant recall. Fortunately the lovely Mrs Cooke, who later visited me at Portal, was, in retrospect, very amused by the incident.

When the weather improved, Sid and I took off on one of the very inexpensive European city weekend specials, widely advertised in *The Sunday Times* travel section. Sid fancied Amsterdam, a European capital he had never visited before.

For something like twenty-five quid we flew over on a regular flight and stayed at a comfortable three-star hotel. Sid never actually believed it would be so cheap, he was waiting for the hidden extras to appear, which of course did not. I had boasted of a four-night stay in Moscow with a group of twelve friends on a regular flight, staying at the usual Russian Intourist hotel for an unbelievable twenty-nine pounds which was around seventy-five dollars then. Admittedly it was cold, like fifteen below, but a great weekend was had by all. When I think back that this was only eleven years ago, I can't believe it myself. Needless to say the offer is now closed.

Amsterdam charmed Sid, the architecture, good Indonesian food, marvellous museums and fascinating bookshops. We wandered into the perfectly preserved Tuchinski art-Deco cinema which has been used daily since the twenties but looks like it was opened yesterday. It boasts two immaculate period cinema organs in full song. He was fascinated by the early eighteenth century tobacconists staffed by old Dutchmen who look like they had served their apprenticeship in the same store. Tobacco is taken so seriously by the Dutch especially good cigars which are treated with as much reverence as wine is in Britain, a *mishegaas* which kept Sid chuckling.

Mike Van Bloemen's father invited us to lunch on his cosy houseboat. Being a literary man, he and Sid hit it off. Sid must have eaten five pounds of the scrumptious Dutch dark chocolate over the weekend, like a schoolboy who has found a fiver, he dived in and out of sweet shops surveying the goodies with a Billy-Bunter-like eagerness, fixing his eye on the wide selection of brands available. Usually a plump and jolly Dutch lady behind the counter offered Sid small samples of sweets and chocolates to taste. Sid munched and eyed an ample bosom appreciatively.

Our early evening trip to Amsterdam's famous red-light district was fascinating. The voluptuous painted ladies seated enticingly in the windows of charming old houses are a unique display of merchandise.

Fortunately I managed to drag him away from the girls and goo with tempting tales of Carole Shuter and her cream cakes. These delectable concoctions baked by the equally delectable Carole herself were (and still are) served Sundays with lots of other lunchtime goodies at the off-beat Mrs Beaton's Restaurant in Richmond. When Sid was loose on Sunday and usually after my jazz gig we would Porsche westwards to nearby Richmond. A great Sunday afternoon *schmie*, plenty of antique shops and bookstores plus Carole's fancies. At that time we had to shoehorn ourselves into what looked like a crypt to consume the 'fare'. But tantalizing glimpses of Carole's *tusch* as she squeezed past made the cramped conditions almost a pleasure.

Invariably on our return we would call on Walter and Geraldine Houser for a cup of tea. Sid, Wally and I had a mutual devotion to such important film personalities as Vera Hruba Ralston and Elisha Cooke Jnr. Sadly neglected by film buffs, it was, we felt, our duty to remind the world of the pleasures that these worthy citizens of the movie fraternity had provided us with in a bygone era. Wally and I of course were founder members of both the Vera Hruba Ralston and Elisha Cooke Jnr Appreciation Societies. So when such a distinguished literary and film-world figure as S. J. Perelman accepted our invitation of honorary membership we were deeply moved. Sid actually signed the Society's black and white glossy photographs that Wally keeps in a locked strong box under his bed.

One particularly balmy Sunday afternoon in the mid-seventies Geraldine was serving us tea in the back garden. Sid was gently perspiring and seated in the shade under a small verandah. The three of us were engaged in a particularly elusive silver screen conundrum.

'I know, I know, it was Bert Laverne or something like that, I can picture him how, he was British.'

'No it wasn't it was a name like Byron McByrne kind of Hollywood-Celtic. I should know,' said Sid, 'he was in a movie called *My Sister Eileen*, which was about my sister-in-law Eileen McKinney, Nathaniel West's wife.' A momentary diversion was created when Sid produced an old horn-handled penknife.

'In fact,' he said, 'this knife belonged to Nat West'. Walter examined the revered object with interest.

'I've owned it since his death almost forty years ago,' said Sid with obvious pride.

Sipping our tea we continued with the infuriating game, suddenly the name flashed into my mind.

'It's . . .' I was stopped in mid-sentence by a sudden squawk from Sid.

'What the hell was that?'

On his balding pate was a wet brown gritty substance already dribbling down his face on to the front of his open necked shirt. A giggle was heard from the balcony above where a small Houser child was seen holding a glass jug of water from which he had obviously been pouring copious quantities over a droopy potted geranium. Sid by now had removed his grimy spectacles, and a furious Wally had rushed inside the house, tossed me a towel for Sid and raced upstairs to remove the offending babe.

Sid, whose love for young children was similar to my own — minimal, all they do is want — sat alternatively glaring, cleaning his specs, and wiping himself down. Soon a red-eyed child was brought down by Wally, stood in front of Sid and told to say, 'I am sorry'. Sid doing his best to appear unruffled managed a forced smile and patted the little lad on the head. More tea was produced, embarrassment turned into laughter and I was just about to reveal all in the name game when Sid suddenly leapt off his chair like a rip-rap.

'Not again, the little . . .'

The last bit was drowned out by a roar from Wally as he tore upstairs and on to the balcony. This time no child was proffered to apologize, the wails coming from a rear room testified to his personal feelings about the matter. Sid was not so easily appeased this time, even my attempt at resurrecting the 'game' was not brilliantly successful.

'It was Brian Ahearne,' I said with some aplomb.

'Yep,' snapped Sid as he strode toward the bathroom.

Walter gave no response whatsoever.

Chapter 7

Once again the Troubadour pops up. Mike and Sheila were organizing a bunch of regulars to go on another winter break cheapie trip and asked me to join them. As it was to Tunisia and I fancied a return visit I mentioned it to Sid, who also liked the idea. The ridiculous price of twenty-five pounds for five days and nights in Tunisia with or without Dizzy Gillespie, was definitely a royal *mitzeah*. Mike was fed up with attempting to collect money from everyone so gave us the agent's name and address. Sid had already made up his mind it was 'too good to miss'.

So, the next day I visited Mr Petel at 'Jolly Good Time Holidays'. The dank Soho basement belied the company name, but for twenty-five quid what the hell, so I handed over the spondulicks.

At the very last moment, and after several changes of mind my old shipmate, now Barrister and Member of Parliament, Arthur Davidson, decided to join us. Well, actually he almost didn't. Arriving somewhat breathlessly at the railway station (en route for the airport) wearing white plimsolls and toting a hastily packed canvas bag out of which protruded a tennis racket.

After a hideous three hours spent rubbing shoulders and other parts of our anatomy with the hoipolloi and their sticky smelly offspring. We spent a further three hours winging our way to Monastir. The hotel was passable but the totally inedible cous-cous served by an unshaven Arab lackey reminded Sid of past throw-up meals on his favourite steamer the SS Moribunda. So, despite our weary limbs and still clutching our Entro Vioform tablets we made a quick foray to the local kebab shop where another Ali Baba served us great nosh. The following day we arrived in Sousse, and with Sid doing a passable impersonation of W. C. Fields ('The name is Soussé') we entered the Sousse Palace.

Not bad at all, perhaps 'Palace' was something of an

The *schlock* of Sid's dreams.

Sid's close friend, the sweet-meat seller.

overstatement but the rooms were clean and the showers worked. Sid was in a mischievous mood as with Arthur and me he explored the Casbah, losing ourselves in the odorous alleyways of the Arab section.

After stopping at numerous sweetmeat stalls and fingering through mountains of leather and pottery artefacts Sid got tired of repulsing Arab traders and brushing begging children from his sleeves.

'Let's go back to the Palace for a *schlof*,' he suggested. I agreed and we made our way out of the labyrinth to the main drag where we found Mike and Sheila plus friends also looking for a taxi. All the taxis were tiny ancient Renault 750s in which two passengers are a crowd. About six people forced themselves into the front Renault and we three got into the rear car. As the front one crawled away from the curb, ends knocking, smoke pouring from the exhaust, our driver asked Sid in fractured English:

'Where go meester?'

Sid cried, 'Follow that cab!' The driver didn't move.

'Come on buddy, step on the gas,' said Sid.

Arthur interjected with 'Palace Hotel' and off we moved. A disconsolate Sid was mumbling something about, 'Been awaiting the opportunity to say that for forty years and this dummy doesn't understand English'.

Refreshed after our *schlof* we took a stroll around the French section of town and wandered into the Mono Prix, a kind of gallic Woolworths. Arthur stopped at a perfumery counter, peered at a three-foot high pyramid of Roger Gallet *eau de cologne* on special offer, did some quick mental arithmetic and decided it was too much of a bargain to be missed. Intending to pay for it at the cash desk Arthur absent-mindedly plucked a bottle from the heap in front of him. With a horrendous crash the entire pyramid collapsed on to the tiled floor. Amidst a pile of broken glass and torrents of *eau de cologne* Arthur stood white-faced and transfixed. The odour was overpowering and in a flash half the people in the crowded store seemed to converge around poor Arthur.

Sid standing alongside me shrieked, 'Head for the hills,' and scuttled off towards the door. Fortunately, for Arthur the accusing crowd thinned out quickly as the alert young French

42

store manager raced to the disaster area. Efficiently, he conducted Arthur and me to his office where an explanation was demanded. His English was excellent and he sympathized with Arthur's predicament, who together with his profuse apologies offered full payment for all the damage he had caused due to his lack of thought. The young man would not hear of it.

'You are customers at our store and visitors to our country,' he said, 'and accidents do happen.'

'A very civilized young man,' said Arthur sheepishly as we slunk out of the store. Sid who was seated at an adjacent café drinking coffee and smoking a cigarette hailed us as we emerged.

'They tell me a Tunisian Calaboose ain't so bad,' he chuckled as he ordered coffee for us, 'and anyhow Arthur as you would have conducted your own trial I assure you it would only have been a minimal sentence, no more than a year. Two at the most.'

Now somewhat recovered Arthur was beginning to enjoy the ridiculous experience as much as we were.

Later that afternoon my partner Lionel Levy and his lady, Karen, who were staying at nearby Hammamet drove over to dine with us. The 'package' they were part of included accommodation in a kind of third-class Arab holiday camp, Lionel's scathing description of the facilities and Arthur's 'horror-of-the-day' story kept all of us in great explosions of mirth throughout the evening.

The beat up Peugeot we hired for our next day's expedition would have given Mr Hertz apoplexy. Despite the garage owner's assurances that 'It iz a beautiful car, lak new'. We had been told of an early (very early, 5 am) Bedouin market at an oasis about thirty kilometres out in the desert. We duly shook, rattled and rolled ourselves across the dunes with nary a sign of Victor McLaglan, Gary Cooper or even Laurel and Hardy.

The picturesque market was a biblical throwback; the costumes of the nomads, the braying donkeys, and camels clustered around the palm trees at the edge of the pool. Dozens of women were sitting on sacks offering all kinds of produce. Fierce-looking men were haggling over whatever they haggle over. There were rug and brown pottery vendors, and heaps of Arab garments made of heavy blanket cloth (jalliburs) and sundry pathetic piles of smelly tattered, very used, clothing all around. Plus a few ancient trucks laden with aluminium and plastic eating utensils. The sun had risen by the time we arrived but it was still quite cold. The clear light heightened the earthy colours. Tourists were scarce around the area in January so when our group arrived closely followed by a crumpled bus bearing Mike, Sheila and retainers, we were mobbed by laughing children. However, unlike the Souk traders in town, the Bedouins did not pester us. I noticed some women sitting on a very mucky but wonderfully coloured old blanket. When I offered to buy it from them they obviously thought I was *meshugge* when I could have bought a new one for the same price. Although it stank, having received more than its fair share of camel dung in its day, I shoved it in the car trunk and had it washed back in Sousse where it soon dried in the sunshine. I still have it, the colours are superb. Sid, in the meantime was enjoying a haggle with a jolly jallibur vendor over the price of a Ku-Klux-Klan-looking robe. Trying it on over his English tweed sports coat he decided it was too heavy and coarse for him to wear as a bathrobe, but not before I got a photo of him as a latter-day Lawrence. We breakfasted on dates, cakes and coffee at a nearby village where we rendezvoused with Lionel and Karen.

A wonderful day was spent exploring Roman amphitheatres and villas. I remember an especially beautiful display of mosaics featuring fantastic mythological creatures. Sid still on the lookout for a bargain inspected all the grubby bits and pieces offered to him by Arab children. Eventually a smooth-talking guide latched on to him, firstly trying him out with four different languages before deciding he must be American.

'You no look like American Meester, you kidding eh?'

'No, goddammit,' growled Sid. 'You wanna see my passport? Now beat it.' Unperturbed the guide continued his grilling.

'What you do Meester?' Sid ignored him and tried a change of direction, but to no avail, the little man caught up with him and fired more questions at him.

'You doctor?' Sid was blank. 'You teacher?'

Sid turned to Arthur who was walking behind him.

'How do I get rid of this jerk?' he appealed.

Arthur was chuckling so much he could hardly answer Sid who said, 'What's so funny? I could be stuck with him for the rest of our stay in Tunisia'.

Arthur jokingly suggested to Sid that if he actually told him what his occupation was he might go away. The noonday sun and Sid's heavy tweeds did nothing to cool his anger but after some hesitation he turned to the grinning Arab by his side and hissed at him.

'What's your name?'

'Name Meester?'

'Yes name,' said Sid.

'My name is Sid.'

Arthur and I joined Sid in the peals of laughter that followed, the 'guide' who had no idea what we were laughing at joined in the merriment. But sensing that he had won us over somehow offered to take us to the secret tombs and sell us very rare, valuable Roman coins very cheap.

'I am guide,' he kept repeating and took from inside his grubby robe an old leather bag. He emptied several coins into Sid's outstretched palm. Sid turned to me.

'Uric what do you think of these?' I examined them and said I thought they were genuine but not necessarily valuable.

After ten minutes hot haggling in which Sid reduced Sid's opening price from twenty to four dollars, a deal was clinched and Sid was becoming quite chummy with the little fellow. We allowed him to show us the tombs; genuine they were, secret hardly so. Before we drove on to a nearby town for a kebab, Sid had warmed enough to the 'guide' to have told him he was a writer and like him, named Sid. The 'guide' was obviously proud of his newly found namesake and asked him for a photograph and a card (he showed Sid a well-thumbed selection of foreign visitors cards he kept in a folder). Although Sid could not comply with Sid's first request he did fish out a card for him and parted amiably.*

After another couple of days of kebabs, kebabs and more kebabs (the cous-cous tasted like desert sand), Sid was beginning to have hallucinations again, visions of chopped

---

* Six years later Max Wilks' son was approached by a guide in Tunisia who after the usual conversation asked him if he knew his good friend, an American writer named Sid. He then produced a filthy SJP card.

liver, sweet and sour cucumber, alternating between his cravings for Arab sweets. Returning to the hotel after a last-minute shopping expedition I noticed Sid's right arm dart out like a viper's tongue as we passed a barrow of sweets, grabbing a handful he stuffed them in his mouth without changing pace. After a couple of moments of frantic chewing he swallowed hard, looked at me and grinned mischieviously.

The flight back to England was another nightmare. Only relieved by the company and Sheila's idea that all of us in the Troubadour group should do a souvenir drawing. Sid complied and proved that after so many years he still retained some of his cartoonist skills, by producing an excellent caricature. The January fog diverted the plane to Birmingham, so we wound up on a cold and miserable bus journey back to London during which neither Sid, Arthur or I despite singing several rousing choruses of the Slim Gaillard classic, *Flat Foot Floogie and the Floydoy*, could revive the party's flagging spirits.

Chapter 8

I began to notice around then that Sid was becoming disillusioned with his London existence. Nothing I could be specific about, just a general feeling that his enthusiasm was on the wane and his anger towards the lack of enjoyable local facilities was gnawing at him. Places like Parsons on the Fulham Road in which he had liked to eat and keep his eye on the trendy young popsies provoking me into action with sudden suggestions as to how we could pick up a couple of sweet young things at the adjoining table. I would reply that as I was as old as their father, he their grandfather, maybe we should skip the idea.

He would snap back, 'Never too old for a bit of nooky,' and then, 'Let's get out of here Uric. They call this crazy caterwauling, music?'

He was getting restless, but still enjoyed visiting friends like writer/journalist Norman Lewis and family. I would drive him to Lewis's home in the picturesque Essex village of Finchingfield where he listened to stories of Norman's numerous global escapades. Sid enjoyed being in the company of seasoned world travellers. In London we would pop over to the Liebersons where Sandy would keep Sid in touch with recent Hollywood and British film productions. And where (like the Wilks' house) people would just drop in for a little *schmooze* 'n' booze.

A young friend of mine, Peter Nahum, one of Sotheby's art experts lived out in Hertfordshire where at the time his mother, Faith owned a superb black and white timbered Elizabethan manor house, Queen's Hoo. This gem of early English architecture and its charming gardens delighted Sid. He was fascinated by the fact that after four hundred years it was still in use as a family dwelling and not as a museum. Much of the furniture and even some bits of the decoration were original.

Despite these pleasant diversions and our own

companionship Sid's restlessness continued. He missed New York and found the inspiration for his writing not forthcoming in London. So, gradually as he became more depressed he made his decision to return to the States. One of the incidents that saddened me most at this time was a call from him to come over one evening. He was obviously distressed and looked weary and, unusually for him, unkempt. I suggested that we should walk over to the Polish place for a *borscht*, but no gleam came into his eyes, he just said he wasn't hungry.

Pointing to his well-filled bookshelves he said, 'Select a few books for yourself Uric, I am selling the lot tomorrow. What do I need all this junk for? It's becoming a burden'.

I was astonished, 'Sid,' I appealed, 'these are your tools and old friends, don't part with them'.

'Look,' he said, 'I've taken out a couple of dozen I really need, the rest go, a South Kensington dealer is coming to give me a price tomorrow.'

He was very despondent, but continued, 'Also I want you to take my jazz records and some personal items I don't require'.

Again I pleaded, 'Sid you just can't give away your treasured possessions'.

He mumbled, 'Just take 'em, I will see you tomorrow'.

The next night I called around with a Blyume's salt-beef sandwich and a sweet 'n sour. He was in a brighter mood and wolfed them down with a beer.

'I feel better now the books have gone,' he said.

'Not me,' I said.

He replied, 'They were not on your back'.

We talked about the price he got which he admitted was low but the best he could get in a hurry. I knew it was no use arguing with him in his present state of mind but determined to contact Max Wilk as soon as possible. Max would attempt to buy some volumes back from the dealer.†

It was around this period that Sid first mentioned 'The Screen'. Describing to me in glowing terms the magnificently painted hand-made screen he had purchased on his last visit to

† Some books were retrieved, however Sid had great difficulty in getting his money from the dealer. It required solicitor's letters and effort. He received the full amount owing over a year later.

India, a great work of art carried out by the traditional craftsmen of Hindustan on six folding panels.

He assured me he had acquired an incredible bargain for the paltry sum of one hundred dollars plus packing and shipping. Due to its size, over six foot by three foot, and not inconsiderable weight it was thought better to send it by sea. Unless of course one was in the habit of doling out king's ransoms, which Sid decidedly was not. After months of waiting and Sid's dispatching of several letters to the source which included photostats of his receipt and threats of action, none of which, needless to say, were ever replied to, Sid had a call from a shipping office agent in the city. They had a crate awaiting his collection after it had passed through customs.

'Customs?' queried Sid. 'But it's not liable to duty.'

'Well you can't tell,' replied the agent. 'They might consider it to be a luxury item, subject to full duty or an essential household item at a lower rate.'

Sid spluttered, 'Tell them it is a work of art, cost almost nothing and is not subject to duty'.

The agent promised to do his best. Sid sweated it out for a few days until the agent called to impart the gloomy news.

'Mr Perelman, I paid the customs thirty pounds duty on your behalf, now where do you wish the crate delivered to?'

Sid swallowed hard as he gave his address.

'Let me see,' said the agent, 'that will be twenty pounds for delivery.'

'What?' shrieked Sid. 'I understood the shipping charges which I paid in India included delivery to my door.'

'No sir,' said the agent. 'They include shipping dock to dock and my clearance fees, it was clearly written in the contract you signed in Calcutta. When I receive your cheque for fifty pounds the screen will be delivered immediately.'

Sid reluctantly surrendered, still considering the screen to be a *mitzeah* at more than double the initial price he had paid for it. Unfortunately the crate was delivered on Mr Withers' day off and during the quarter of an hour when a starving Sid had popped down to the 'deli' for a rye bread after having waited in almost all day.

He found it in the porch propped against the wall and almost blocking the front door entirely. The porter in the next block who had signed for it agreed after a little monetary persuasion to help place it in a rear entrance passageway in Sid's house. This did not exactly enhance ingress and egress but Sid had little alternative.

A few days after delivery Sid received a polite note from the estate agents who managed the building, asking him to move the crate as soon as possible as there had been complaints. It was at this juncture that he told me of this eighth wonder of the world and his predicament as to where it should reside until he could find the place of honour it deserved. When I asked to view it he told me that as it was in six parts which required assembling, he thought it better not to remove it from the substantial crate as yet, because it would be a bugger to repack. Things became desperate when about two weeks later, he received by hand another letter telling him to remove the crate forthwith otherwise it would be removed and sent to storage at his expense. Over a corned beef and cucumber he elaborated on his dilemma.

By this time he had decided on returning to New York and felt that perhaps the screen was now superfluous to his new minimum goods and chatels image, and did I know of an

This garage was close by Sid's flat, enabling him to keep it under close surveillance.

antique dealer or interior decorator whom he could offer it to for a pretty penny. Adding with a wink that I might be able to make a nice chunk of small change in the way of introductory commissions. In the meantime, if he paid for a van and driver could I find a temporary home for it in my place. Although I did not relish the idea I considered Sid's present unhappy plight and agreed that it could be put in an empty basement flat (to which I had a set of keys) in the house where I lived. So the next day it was put in the empty flat.

Despite several joint attempts to sell it including a glowing advert in a glossy interior decorators' magazine nobody showed even a flicker of interest. Then, one day I was notified by my landlord that the basement flat was to be redecorated prior to sale and would I move the large box. Once again Sid was in *schtuck* with the screen but after a few days a fresh solution loomed. A friend of a friend of his had a garage in Ealing where his wife kept her Mini. He thought it would fit in easily if Sid could arrange to get it to the address. Another ten pounds for transport and hey presto the screen arrived in Ealing. Either the crate was larger or the garage smaller than described because when the lady put her Mini inside there was very little clearance.

All appeared peaceful on 'The Screen Front' for a few weeks then Sid had a call from his friend's friend telling him that due to a favour he had done for a complete stranger the doors of his wife's Mini were beginning to look like a dodgem car. Sid apologized profusely and promised to have the crate removed. Once again on 'The Screen Hotline' Sid desperately sought a solution.

'Uric, what the fuck can I do now?' he beseeched.

'Hold on Sid,' I said. 'I think Peter Nahum has got a garden shed and he lives quite near Ealing.'

'Tell him I will be his slave for ever,' said Sid as I called Peter.

Not only did Peter take the screen but he wangled free transport. Sid was extremely grateful for the haven but at the same time very concerned about the ultimate deterioration of his valuable work of art in an obviously damp garden shed. So, under Sid's supervision Peter and I studiously wrapped the crate in plastic. Over a cup of tea Sid asked Peter why Sothebys would not accept the screen. Peter explained that as a 'modern work' it might not fetch as much as he expected. Sid obviously thinking about how much the screen had cost him so far gloomily accepted this. So, like a gravestone the plastic-wrapped crate was laid to rest in Peter's shed.

After the 'usual' statutory period a brand new development occurred. It seems that Peter and Caroline had placed their house on the market several months earlier but buyers were scarce in the early seventies and so far there had been no response. At least not until the day after the screen had been delivered. When the agent called to say he had a prospect who subject to inspection would be interested in immediate purchase. Fortunately for the Nahums, unfortunately for Sid, a deal was a deal, and was consummated within the month. An apologetic Peter broke the news to a despairing Sid who this time did not bother even to tell me. He dragged Max Wilk into the arena. Max had already sensed that he was to be the next link in 'The Screen Saga' so was not entirely unprepared for Sid's tale of woe.

'OK,' he agreed. 'I've got a lumber room. If you've got transport, you've got space.' My feeling of euphoria created by the severance of my own connections with the screen was speedily demolished by a call from Sid. He asked me if I could find some transport, as the guys he had previously used appeared to have gone out of business. The following weekend, therefore, driving a friend's estate car I arrived at the Nahums. After an heroic and sweaty tussle with ropes and clips we got the screen fixed on the roof rack. Just a traffic-clogged trip across London and we arrived at Max's home. Everybody in the vicinity happened to have a bad back at that moment so painfully Max, Sid and I *schlepped* it up to the attic. Later, suitably refreshed by Barbara, Sid was noticeably calmer as he sighed, 'I should have brought it here in the first place'.

To which I replied, 'Amen brother, Amen'.

The twists and turns along the pathways of life are unpredictable. Yes, you've guessed it, this was not the final resting place of 'The Wandering Screen'. No way.

A certain Mrs Pollock from whom the Wilks had rented their house for an unspecified period suddenly decided she wanted her house back within three months. Under the circumstances

Max and Barbara decided to return to Westport, Connecticut. They, of course, gave Sid ample warning of their decision and asked him to remove the screen as soon as possible.

So, once again at his wit's end, he asked for my help. Just as I was telling him to either pay the exorbitant sum required for shipping it to America or give it away, a sort of joint solution/ miracle occurred. An American lady friend of Sid's had recently married and the couple had purchased Sid's old place in Bucks County. The lovely lady was in London and purchased a piece of antique furniture from me and several other large items which she was planning to ship home. Sid conveniently got a brainwave. He had promised the couple a belated wedding present and here was the perfect solution to his problem. The screen was appreciatively accepted by the lady and shipped with her other purchases in a special container.

Later that year Sid saw for himself 'The Screen Fully Assembled' in all its glory, installed in his old homestead.

Chapter 9

As the time grew nearer to Sid's departure his light heartedness reappeared. A collection of his most recent works had just been published in USA and despite the fact that he already had around sixteen volumes to his credit, plus hundreds of pieces published in *The New Yorker, Travel and Leisure* and elsewhere, he always got a kick out of his latest book.

I helped him sort out and pack in a steamer trunk what was left of his library. He handed me an inscribed original Mickey Mouse frame given to him in 1939 by Eileen McKinney (Nathaniel West's wife) who was Walt Disney's personal assistant at that time. I was most touched and still treasure it greatly.

Somehow I eventually became the go-between for him and the numerous second-hand furniture dealers he had contacted to dispose of his furniture, sundries and enormous work desk. He already saw himself as a man with only a minimal amount of possessions. He had disciplined himself to be ruthless where sentiment and nostalgia were concerned. He did, however, experience some self-recrimination after his return to New York and told me that certain personal items he had handed to me were in my custody, not my possessions. These he collected in due course.

Shortly before his departure a bunch of us spent a hilarious evening in the East End squashed into two cars. We firstly ate at the ancient, filthy underground tavern 'Dirty Dicks', then drove out to Edmonton, losing ourselves in a rain storm looking for a certain pub cum club where the legendary British music hall comic Max Wall was making a rare appearance. Wall, now well into his seventies, has long been regarded as one of Britain's zaniest and offbeat comics. Sid was very impressed and I took him backstage to say hello to Wall, who was equally impressed to meet Perelman having been an admirer of his work for years.

The following week, Troubadour Mike and Sheila gave a small going-away party for Sid. Most of his intimate British friends attended and Sid was his perky self once more, assuring us all that, although he was moving home, he would be back and forth crossing the Atlantic like it was his own swimming pool. With a lady friend of mine, Terry Boase, who was one of Sid's favourites, I saw him off on the Southampton boat train.

Of course I missed him, despite both our idiosyncracies we had a close affection. Perhaps we had a mutual appreciation of each other's *haimischer* qualities: a love of women, though of a totally different type; an appreciation of and reluctance to part with money easily; a love of literature and wit, an ability to observe keenly and above all a sense of the ridiculous. I soon received a letter from him telling me that he was installed at an East 75th Street apartment and that the absence of London power cuts was not bothering him at all but the New York 95° temperature outside was. We exchanged letters regularly, his two or three pages of single-space type on *The New Yorker* stationery were usually hilarious if somewhat esoteric.

Within three months of resettling in New York his itchy feet began to erupt so when the former editor of *Travel and Leisure* suggested a two-month trip out East he jumped at it. Apart from Indonesia and Japan and the Seychelles he also visited two of the obscure and staggeringly beautiful Himalayan kingdoms in the vicinity of Bhutan.

Returning early '73 to New York via London. I booked him in for a few days at his old favourite, the venerable Brown's Hotel in Albemarle Street, just around the corner from the gallery. It was great to *schmooze* again and watch him stoke up at Blyumes.

I gave a little get-together at my flat for Sid and buddies, we also had a meal with publisher Tom Maschler, his wife Fay and her sister Beth Coventry. Beth was one of Sid's favourite English ladies. Olga Deterding, the eccentric Shell heiress, gave one of her periodic celebrity-packed soirées to which I dragged Sid. He was, of course, fascinated by the whole mélange of British 'with it' society. Left over from the swinging sixties in crazy costume, they ranged from hippy to Harrods, actress to bishop, gay to gorilla, with Olga lounging in filmy negligée amongst a crowd of 'would be', 'could be' and 'should bes' of all shapes, sizes, ages and sexes. The atmosphere reminded Sid of the many Hollywood orgies he had attended in the thirties. Both Olga and her parties were unique.

Some six months passed before Sid set foot again on our damp terrain. I met him at Heathrow and drove him to Browns. As we entered the lobby to a chorus of greetings from the manager and staff, Sid discovered his notecase was missing from his pocket. Obviously very distressed about this he decided we must return to the airport immediately as he remembered leaving it in the callbox from which he had telephoned me. Not a hope in hell of getting it back now I thought as I gunned the Porsche westward. Whether Sid's tense expression was due to the 120 mph on the speedo or his missing notecase I am not sure as he remained silent all the way. Leaping out of the parked car he ran towards the callbox, returning a few minutes later grinning.

'I am in *mazel*,' he said. 'Would you believe it? Still on the floor.' I said I thought he was very lucky.

'Let's try to keep it that way,' he replied. 'We are not in a hurry to get back, don't you have speed limits over here?' I took the hint.

Back at Browns, he called around making sure his pals were aware that 'Sid was in Town'. Chaim Raphael would journey from Brighton. Alan Coren would invite him to one of the infamous *Punch* lunches. He would make a dinner date with book agent Pat Kavanagh, call Mel Calman, and so on and so forth. Sid adored these action-packed short visits to London.

I was unfortunately unable to spend much time with him as within a few days I left on one of my own Third World jaunts to Ethiopia. A fascinating land which, alas, since the demise of Emperor Haille Selassie has been troubled. We did, however, manage a Sunday trip. I found a couple of young girls, an English rose for Sid and an oriental beauty for myself. As they would be wasted crammed into the rear of the Porsche I hired a somewhat larger car for our day out to Southampton water where my ex-partner and old friend Alan Jacobs and his son, were about to sail off on a crazy voyage in a catamaran.

Alan is one of those guys who can do anything which

requires manual skill, he also has rare additional qualities like a highly developed sense of humour and love of literature, which was much appreciated by Sid. Alan and I had, for five years prior to my entering the art world, a good time buying vintage cars, which he would fix and I would sell. It's not often one sees an oily hand appear from beneath a Lagonda reaching for a bagel with chopped herring. Alan and I had enjoyed many adventures. Then shortly after our partnership ended Alan got badly smashed up which necessitated several months in hospital and a great deal of surgery. Alan was a tough guy, he resisted acute pain and gradually recovered about ninety per cent of his physical activeness. In fact, in the mid-sixties he joined the enigmatic John Warth and myself at the insane Portobello Motor Company. A business side-venture, evolved during a motor trip to India which was captained by Warth to search for vintage automobiles belonging to impecunious maharajahs. The Portobello venture was tremendous fun if not so financially viable. Every Saturday at a vintage car zoo, Jacobs, Warth, Lister and Levy would be chatting up the swinging sixties crowd, trying to sell them an ancient Chrysler (cashing in on the Bonnie and Clyde craze) or a trendy French dustbin called a Citroen 2 CV or even a Warth ancient Rolls Royce or Big Cat C-type Jaguar. We probably carried the most offbeat stock of motor cars in Britain until, due to property speculators, we were kicked out of the premises and forced to close around 1969. Not, however, before Sid had spent several hours hanging around, earwigging the sales talk and lapping up the Marx Brothers atmosphere. Our *Motor Sport* adverts became instant classics, for example:

1929 Mercedes SSK 250 supercharged touring car as new.
Offers invited for this unwanted barmitzvah present.

It was a couple of years after the Portobello demise that Alan Jacobs was offered a job managing a BMW agency in Jamaica. This coincided with his recent desire to become a sailor. So, acquiring a second-hand catamaran and fixing it up, he announced his intention to sail to Jamaica accompanied only by his fifteen-year-old son and forgoing such luxuries as radios and modern navigational aids.

Sid and myself, and the girls inspected Alan's tiny craft in disbelief.

'You sure you mean the Atlantic and not the Channel,'

asked Sid.

Alan was cool, confident, and casual about his intended departure the following day.*

I am certain that Sid was in good hands for the remainder of his stay as his close friend Harvey Orkin was around. On the several occasions that Harvey and I had arranged a get-together things had gone 'phut', so, to my regret, we never did meet. His premature death was a blow to Sid who regarded him as a very special pal with an underrated talent.

Early in 1974 Sid wrote to me from Florida suggesting that I join him and friends Lillian Hellman, and Francis and Albert Hackett at a luxurious house they had rented for the winter in Saratoga.

Initially it sounded like most people's idea of paradise (actually not my scene at all) with its own motorboat on the quay, a swimming pool and late model car. Also, included in the deal were a young couple who acted as housekeepers, and a pet cat. Sid's description of the weather at the time of writing was somewhat daunting, pelting rainstorms and frigid temperatures. I wrote back to him suggesting that he hop on a plane to London where we were expecting a pleasant warm, mild and dry winter. His second Florida dispatch was even gloomier, since Lillian Hellman had left for New York (she couldn't stand the place) the cooking had deteriorated drastically. The housekeeper's wife was a specialist with dumplings and boiled cabbage but eight times a week was enough already. He described the local rye bread as the brainchild of a mad scientist. The local store stocked nothing but striped nylon sun-loungers and his two months at the villa was like paying a bit part in *The Night of the Iguana*.

What a relief it must have been for him to return to the dirty, noisy, ice-bound 'Apple'. A couple of weekends with Max and Barbara and friend Terry Rice out in Westport nourished and revitalized him.

Due to a swift decision on my part to act the part of a dull businessman in a short film Bob Gill was making for Holiday

---

* For the record, he was blown off course after about six incident-packed weeks. Landed in Antigua; loved the island, so stayed on where he resides to this day.

Inn I got to see Sid in New York a few months later. The movie was a fourteen-day dash between Holiday Inns in London, Beirut, Byblos, Zurich, Bruges, Brussels, London, New York, Niagara Falls, Toronto, Chicago, Memphis, Miami and Barbados where a breathless Gill left me and the other actors lolling with fatigue. I managed to get a few days rest with Alan Jacobs in Antigua where Alan is known locally as 'Dr Jacobs, dee man dat fixes dee boats'. I called Sid and he took me around his New York 'delis'. I also met briefly his son Adam.

By this time Sid had moved to his final residence. The Gramercy Park Hotel, a place he had known for years and felt at home in. He had a comfortable suite, excellent service and I agreed that it made a lot of sense. He was intrigued with my brief film career. Telling me that he had always thought there was a notable thespian, possibly the equal of Sir Laurence or Sir John G. concealed behind my craggy facade.

His big news was that he had recently been tied up with the production of his own play, *The Beauty Part*. It had opened in New York and he liked the results. Although it had received mixed reviews, three of them, in *Newsweek*, the *Daily News* and *The New Yorker,* were excellent. I myself had read the script and found it an hilarious plot, but for some pecular reason involved with theatre the play did not take off.

Chapter 10

A very cheery letter arrived early in '75 to tell me that Sid would be setting his brogues on my patch in March, en route for far-forgotten places again. I was asked to warn them (Blyumes) in Fouberts Place to light a candle under the chicken soup and alert the Shepherds Market popsies to freshen up their make-up. He arrived in a buoyant mood, checked in at Browns looking exceptionally dapper and at least ten years younger than his seventy-two years. He assured me he had fully recovered from a recent ankle sprain after falling out of the sack during a dawn encounter with a young widow.

His global travel plans on behalf of *Travel and Leisure* magazine included Scotland, Paris, Zurich, Russia, Israel, Iran, Kashmir, Pakistan, Borneo and Tahiti. Several of these places he had not previously visited. Within a few days he was off to Edinburgh and points north in search of a revered Scottish castle inhabited by a Laird McSomebody near the village of Auchtertochtie (Well, that's what Sid called it). It appears that the kilted one turned out to be a wet-brained scoundrel who removed several of Sid's dollars through a ridiculous series of contricks that he could hardly believe. On the telephone from Scotland Sid furiously described a hilarious scene where the Laird, after relieving him of ten pounds to buy a desperately require cat basket, parked his van on a 'No Parking' zone in a busy street in Edinburgh, telling Sid he would be back in a few minutes.

'Just popping over the road to the pet shop for pussy's new basket,' he piped! He then disappeared from the face of the earth for three hours leaving Sid to cope with angry traffic wardens and police constables. Vainly trying to explain to each one that he was not the car owner, not did he know where he was but when he did return Sid's wrath would be far worse punishment than any local magistrate could dish out. His rage was compounded by the fact that for some reason unbeknown to Sid, and without him even noticing it, the looney Laird had locked all the van doors from the outside and the locks fitted were special. Poor Sid could not get out without climbing through a narrow window. Because of acute hunger and nature's call Sid was discussing with a traffic warden the possibility of calling a local locksmith when the Laird somewhat inebriated suddenly reappeared, unlocked the door, and ignoring Sid's protests, and the warden's proffered ticket, drove off as quickly as the old hack would move. Sid sat fearfully as the crazy Scot erratically piloted the vehicle back to the eroding family seat. Needless to say, after attending to his needs, Sid packed and called a local taxi to drive him back to Edinburgh.

Following this debacle Sid took off for Paris. I drove over for the long Easter Weekend with Alan Sytner and Jean Elston to join him. Sid was still in a bouncy mood and we enjoyed a few good meals and a visit to an art naïve exhibition in which some of our Portal artists were participating. The formal and pompous attitude of the gallery director almost became a scene from a Jacques Tati movie. Sid curled up in a corner when a small barrel-shaped Monsieur Le Director waddled into the gallery attired in formal morning attire. After I had introduced myself he viewed me through rimless bifocals with obvious disbelief. I then produced my card which he carefully scrutinized before reluctantly extending his hand. Turning around to Sid I introduced him and my party with as much decorum as I could muster (which aint much I can assure you). After a frozen ten minutes we went through a formal departure ceremony and left. I had never seen Sid chuckle so vigorously as he did in the car, removing his spectacles to wipe his eyes.

'Central Casting could not do a job like that,' he said. 'That guy was strictly Emile Zola.'

Over the next few months I received letters from Sid describing his current adventures, including an account of his being hijacked on an Australian flight. Fortunately the thugs were apprehended without injury to anyone aboard. But Sid said the episode did have its sweaty moments.

His short stay in Israel was fraught with aggravation. Paradoxically Perelman and Israel didn't mix. Israel was just too Jewish for Sid, or maybe it wasn't Jewish enough. The result of this extended global galavant was the very funny *Eastward Ha* (Simon and Schuster). Later that year I was invited to visit China with a group of British medical practitioners who were studying acupuncture and Chinese alternative medicine. The invite came through an Anglo/Chinese association and I had been waiting for years to get a reservation. I was working on my first book about British contemporary primitive art at the time and close to the deadline. Therefore I was on the horns of a dilemma (no connection with the bulls of Pamplona), either skip the trip or call in a co-author/editor. I chose the latter. To the detriment of the book but the enhancement of my pleasure.

Sid was rather cynical about my attempts to become an author and wrote a none too complimentary, but very funny parody about me in *The New Yorker*. Later on, however, he did pay me a backhanded compliment by writing in a letter to a friend, praise of an article I had written.

A phone call from Heathrow to ask me to alert the dry cleaner to be ready for a large express consignment was Sid's announcement of his next 'en route' arrival.

He had been up to his usual party tricks and three of the four pairs of pants he carried on the trip were smothered in a variety of liquids and substances, varying from wine to ice-cream. Sid was not a clumsy man but had almost a psychic empathy with wine-spillers, soup-spillers, any kinda-spillers within range of him. Some people have a special magnetism which works within the vicinity of minor misfortunes. Put Sid at a cocktail party, or near a buffet or as a dinner guest and the odds were that during the course of the evening there would be a muttered 'Christ' from Sid as he resignedly wiped something messy from his trousers. I am certain that Nat Zeller, the South Ken 'Little' dry cleaner and presser had missed Sid's business since he had left because he rose valiantly to the call of duty and worked overtime on Sid's pants.

There were no social calls on this forty-eight hour visit but Sid filled me in with tales of his varied experiences. I had always been amused by a story he had told me of some American friends, who years ago on a South American cruise had been served by an efficient and Jewish wisecracking steward. On the last day of the voyage they tipped the steward, whose name was Sid, and asked him for his full name as they intended to do the cruise again next year and wanted to reserve his services.

'Oh just write to the shipping line and ask for S. J. Perelman,' he replied.

'You really mean S. J. Perelman like the writer?' they asked in amazement. 'We are good friends of his.'

'Then your friend must be a phony,' he replied. '*I* am S. J. Perelman the writer.' Whereupon he headed for the galley and did not reappear.

The mystery was never resolved but the real Sid chuckled when he said that one of them must be under an illusion.

Somewhat closer to the genuine article was a character I am very well acquainted with, whose family name Perelman was abbreviated to Pearl. Ben Pearl, an itinerant antique dealer, originated from Liverpool. Around the mid-fifties he became a Troubadour habituée. His ambition was to become an actor-playwright. It was with a profound and photographic knowledge of Shakespeare's dialogue that he punctuated most of his conversations (or should I say monologues). His rich Liverpudlian brogue intermingled with Yiddish gestures, melodramatically spouting Shakespeare was a riot. But it was his own one-act plays that brought him fame along the length and breadth of Old Brompton Road.

'I am Ben Pearl the only play-a-day man,' he would chant. Then, a trifle immodestly and pre-dating Mohammed Ali he would proclaim, 'I am the greatest undiscovered genius that the world of literature has ever known,' to anyone within earshot.

Amongst his undiscovered masterpieces were such 'Jarry-like' classics as, *I've got fivepence in my secret pocket*, and *I carried myself on my own back, I am innocent* (stay away if you have a weak heart), and featuring a character who was a sidekick of Ben's 'The Count in the Russian Overcoat'. These one-act plays had been played by Troubadour regulars in the tiny rear garden strictly for our own pleasure. Mike and Sheila had discovered an offbeat craftsman artist Ralph Bates to paint one of the posters advertising these momentous events. I have retained and framed several of these excellent primitive posters and Sid was intrigued by them. Even more so after I had described my experiences as Ben Pearl's chauffeur, a job which I undertook during a slack period in the late fifties.

In an ancient Ford V8 and wearing a peaked cap I drove Ben at a steady 25 mph (he got hysterical at anything faster) accompanied by his assistant, 'Golden Boy', a city-gent-type Englishman, along the byways of Sussex, Surrey and Kent, awaiting for them to select an elegant residence. There I would stop, and 'Golden Boy' would do his stuff on the knocker arranging for Mr Pearl of Bond Street to view and possibly purchase some of the treasures within.

I had met Ben loping 'Groucho-Marx-like' along Bond Street very recently. After complimenting him on his splendid attire, dog tooth (more like elephant's tooth), multi-coloured tweed jacket, with red carnation, yellow waistcoat, cavalry twill pants, brown boots and topped with a green English snap brim with obligatory side-feathers. I suggested we should meet for lunch soon to which he agreed. As Sid was leaving London on Sunday evening and had no lunch plans I mentioned Ben Pearl. Sid said sure, if he's free let's meet him for lunch. It took me a good ten minutes on the 'phone trying to explain to Ben, who Sid was. He kept interjecting with 'Yeah, yeah, but can he make me famous chief?' When I finally mentioned the Marx Brothers he was obviously impressed as he momentarily stopped interjecting. Like Sid, he loved lethal Jewish food and suggested a *Kosher* emporium on Baker Street. The place was jammed with what looked like the overflow of a *chasidic* convention so, Sid and I, and Ben had to sit on counter-stools separated by one bearded old gent complete with *yarmulkah* who was slurping bean and barley soup. This didn't stop Ben from diving into Sid at full pelt. Raising his voice even louder than usual to counteract the Rabinical din, he delivered a monologue into Sid's right ear about his plan to dethrone Sir Laurence Olivier.

After half an hour of this tirade and lukewarm lumpy *latkes* Sid managed to signal to me his immediate desire to leave by looking at his watch and interrupting Ben.

'My God it's two thirty, I've not packed and must be at the airport by four.' We grabbed the cheque and flew.

Chapter 11

In the spring of the following year Sid suggested by letter that I join him at a villa he had previously stayed in on the Greek island of Rhodes. It was situated in the centre of the small ancient village of Lindos. He painted a glowing picture of its many attractions not the least being in his opinion the hordes of maurauding single young ladies. I readily accepted his invitation not having enjoyed his company for several months. I am not normally in the habit of taking leisure holidays in the sun I prefer busy adventurous trips, but anything could turn into anything when Sid was around.

I visited my old friend Mr Petel having traced him through several new addresses to a lair over a chemist shop in Shepherds Bush. Reminding him of his boast that he could always supply the cheapest airflight ticket, a man of his word, he booked me a flight without delay. Asking myself what would Sid be missing most in Greece I decided it had to be as usual something *haimischer*. So popping in Blyumes, I purchased twelve cans of Bloom's *Kreplach* soup. I did not realize the weight or space problems this nourishment could cause me. Fortunately I was spared having to explain *Kreplach* to a Greek customs official as we were whisked off the plane and on to a bus so quickly that I thought we must have been mistaken for the Melina Mecouri entourage.

Sid and I had a tear-jerking reunion when I almost bumped into him as I was lugging my heavy suitcase door-to-door-salesman style down a narrow cobbled alleyway, trying to follow the bus driver's directions to the villa. A very bronzed Sid nattily attired in white shirt, shorts and sandals, came around the corner carrying a loaf of bread in a string bag. It seemed I had overshot the villa by a couple of hundred yards so had to *schlepp* my case back up the hill. Sid, bright and breezy, showed me my quarters. The villa, which I believe was owned by Germaine Greer, was compact and looked comfortable. It boasted a fine library and a breath-taking view of the nearby beach, where Sid assured me reclined some of the most alluring creatures since Venus. He handed me an enormous pair (wait for it) of naval binoculars to prove his point(s). The cooking and toilet facilities, he explained, seemed to have been tacked on to the building as an afterthought, but one doesn't expect the Waldorf Astoria in Lindos.

'Talking of cooking,' I said, 'I've brought you an offering.'

When it's *kreplach* time in Lindos.

'You shouldn't have, old boy,' he replied. 'What is it?' Whereby I piled the stack of cans on the table. Peering at a label Sid read 'Bloom's *Kreplach* Soup'. He smiled and said, 'You've brought enough to supply the Israeli army'.

'Well,' I said, 'I though maybe we could be innovators and hold Lindos's first *Kreplach* soup and cheese party.'

His suggestion was let's try one out now with the fresh bread. One would think that eating twelve cans of *Kreplach* soup would become somewhat monotonous, but within a week Sid had devoured the lot with obvious pleasure.

By a lucky coincidence the party in the next villa included

66

our mutual friend from London, Beth Coventry. She agreed to cook for the group, but as they all ate out almost every evening in one of the proliferation of noisy but appetizing tavernas, we were able to enjoy Beth's company. Sid knew a few people with places in Lindos and I had already bumped into the lovely Gayle Simpson, so we were assured of interesting company most evenings. One elegant English lady in particular, Mary North who lived in a fascinating old villa and, together with Sandy a lively New Zealand gal, ran a hand-woven fabric shop in the main street. This is where Sid and I hung out most days between trips to the post office waiting for Sid's mail and countless coffees and beers at any one of several cafés (usually the one with the choicest array of blondes on display).

I had already christened Lindos 'Sloane-Square-on-Sea' as most of the popsies spoke with shrill upperclass 'Sloane Ranger' tones. Although Sid was entranced by those willowy English roses with their creamy complexions and fair curls, they had very little allure for me. I found most of them are pretty boring and gauche with little style. My own preference for the 'Annie Hall', New York style girls mystified Sid. Not that either of us scored on that trip. I got my kicks watching the male middle-aged German tourists accompanied by their wives. These guys were salivating over the tantalizing but untouchable girls. The dollies were in turn competing with each other in the amount of flesh they could reveal to the handsome, smelly, ever ogling local Donkey boys, whilst awaiting their whispered propositions.

'Darleeng English gell, I luuv you, I meet you, yes?' The answer was usually in the affirmative.

Sitting in the square one afternoon I watched a heart-rending scene. A bronzed English girl whose time was up, about to depart on the bus to Rhodes airport was clinging tearfully to her Donkey boy. He in turn was smothering her with affection and promises of undying love. Finally the bus arrived, she boarded and was still waving pathetically to him as it disappeared in a dust cloud. Less than ten minutes later a bus load of new talent appeared. Selecting a clone of his previous one-and-only the Donkey boy with his most engaging smile approached her and with a declaration of his genuine love picked up her suitcase and escorted her into a nearby café.

One day as dawn cracked I was awoken by Sid and told to get up and dress quickly, as I was in for a special treat, breakfast at Rhodes. Not quite Tyffanys but at least it could boast of one of the Seven Wonders of the World. To reach this metropolis we were required to ride the local rattlebox of a bus. When this contraption arrived in the square Sid shot off like a bat out of hell, scattering the waiting group of schoolkids, peasants and tourists. He jumped the steps and landed with a plonk in a middle seat. Some three minutes later I managed to squeeze through the crowds to where Sid was beckoning me through the window.

'You've got to get a seat on the opposite side to the sun,' he drawled. I bowed to his greater experience.

After an hour of sickening jolts and lurches we reached the wonderous market place of Rhodes. Sid was eager for us to get breakfast and explore this colourful market and strode off into the crowd.

'Let's get some toast and coffee,' he yelled. 'Follow me.'

The market is littered with cafés of all shapes, sizes and smells. After selecting the cleanest we sat down at a table where Sid asked the smiling waiter for coffee and toast, the waiter's smile turned into a puzzled look.

'Tost, wat ees tost meester?' Sid patiently tried to explain, trying first hot bread, then burnt bread, then grilled bread. The waiter remained puzzled.

'We got bread, no burnt,' he said, adding, 'I breeng you coffee an nice cake, yes?'

'No,' snapped Sid and turning to me, 'Uric let's go, the man's an idiot.'

The second café brought no better results but in the third a grey-haired buxom woman agreed to burn some bread for us.

Five minutes later and after listening to hilarious shrieks coming from the partition which acted as a kitchen, the lady reappeared with four blackened pieces of bread, some goat's cheese, a pot of honey and two cups of coffee. Sid picked up a charred remnant of bread, smeared it with honey and crunched it between his teeth.

'There you are,' he grinned. 'I told you I'd get toast.' I ordered cake.

We walked in the blazing sunshine to a pottery Sid had been told about. We finally found it, closed. A kind old man from next door, noticing our predicament, offered to awaken the potter. So we sat on a bench outside the studio awaiting his arrival. Sid, spot on form, picked the bit of bench with a patch of damp clay on it.

'Lucky I'm wearing my old pants,' he mumbled as he brushed himself off.

The young potter eventually arrived and Sid chose three small pieces which he paid for, had packed, and asked me to carry for the rest of the day. Apart from having to *schlepp* a box of pots around the hot dusty alleyways of Rhodes I enjoyed my 'treat'.

Sid's own treat was a huge bag of oranges which he had suddenly developed a pregnant addiction for, and a selection of anti-mosquito coils to try out that night. The nasty buzzing pests forced us to spray our rooms with a vile liquid or burn the stinking coils. Each evening before retiring we selected the evil of the night. Oh, and the rats! Maybe I'd better not mention them.

On other mornings Sid would spend a couple of hours rattling away on his old portable or fiddling with his Zenith in an attempt to find the 'Voice of America'. Then he would embark on his daily pilgrimage to Mr Papandreas the tailor who worked in a hovel just down the road from the villa. It seems that during his visit to Lindos the year previously Sid had 'discovered' this little man around the corner. He appeared to renovate a couple of Sid's jackets and trousers quite skilfully and inexpensively. So, on this trip as Sid had picked up a lightweight suit length, cheaply in Athens, he handed it to Mr Papandreas reminding him of his last year's promise to make him the best suit he had ever worn at the lowest price. Naturally Mr Papandreas was delighted to welcome back his American friend and client, paying a great deal of attention to getting Sid's measurements accurately.

This measuring-up plus Sid's explicit instructions as to his styling requirements was reinforced by a *New Yorker* advertisement of a nattily dressed gent in a lightweight suit which Sid also passed over to Mr Papandreas with the first of several advance payments. One would have thought that with the amount of time that Sid put in with Papandreas daily that he was being fitted for a coronation robe at least. Sid assured me that Papandreas was an old-time craftsman, and that the time spent, coffee consumed, and cigarettes smoked in his hovel each morning would be worth it when the end product appeared. One afternoon it happened. A smiling Sid appeared on the patio wearing an immaculate jacket. I admitted, after examining the workmanship and excellent fit, that the old fellow was a genuine craftsman.

'How about the pants?' I asked.

'Ready in a couple of days,' said Sid.

As we passed the tailor's shop several times daily Sid and he waved and chatted amiably for a few moments, the conversation ending with the assurance that, 'De pants will be ready tomorrow'.

Towards the end of our stay Sid began to get concerned about the trousers, mentioning to me that he had not actually seen Papandreas working on them. When confronted with this fact Papandreas patted Sid on the back telling him, 'Don't worry day ready for sure'.

Two days prior to our departure Sid was displaying obvious signs of anxiety over the arrival of the trousers. His warm relationship with Mr Papandreas tarnished somewhat when Sid stormed into his shop demanding his trousers forthwith. Unperturbed by Sid's wrath, Papandreas said, 'Go home, one hour Mister'.

We returned to the villa, where to our amazement at the appointed time there was a rap at the door. Sid saw a young boy deposit a plastic carrier bag on the step and run off down the street. Opening the bag Sid hauled out a pair of pants made of the same fabric as his jacket.

'You see,' he said as he turned to me, 'you come on strong, you get results.'

Two minutes later whilst trying them on in the bedroom I heard a groan from Sid.

'Uric come here,' he spluttered.

I entered to find him wearing the pants, which, because of their immense waist measurement he was forced to hold up by hand. Glancing at the lower portions I noticed that the ankles were very unfashionably narrow. Silently he let them drop to the floor and wriggled out of them. Putting on his robe he turned to me.

'What a fucking disaster.'

On retrieving the crumpled heap from the floor I had to admit that they would have been a more suitable fit for Oliver Hardy than Sid.

Siesta or no siesta, within five minutes Sid was hammering on shutters of Papandreas's shop. An impatient Sid continued with the pounding until a tousled Papandreas appeared on the overhanging balcony. Sid holding the trousers towards him, suggesting that they were made for an elephant. In fractured English a cool Papandreas explained that the pants were not made by him.

'What?' exploded Sid. 'I gave you an order for a two-piece suit, not a jacket.'

Once again the old tailor gave a painful explanation.

'De jacket I made good, de pants my brother-in-law make,' adding what might have been a Greek curse on his brother-in-law's name.

The gist of his further message was that he and his unpronounceable brother-in-law had once been partners, each one strictly sticking to his own speciality. Years ago they had an irrevocable dispute and dissolved the partnership. Neither wanted to destroy a thriving business so, they agreed through their wives to continue as suitmakers. Either Papandreas or bother-in-law would pass on the cloth, cash and delivery for the required garment as the case might be. One of their hordes of children or grandchildren acting as go-between. Papandreas then threw up his hands apologetically as he turned to go back inside.

'You and boy go brother-in-law, not me, 'ee make elephant pants.'

At that moment a young boy mysteriously appeared. Beckoning us to follow him. Squeezing past donkeys whilst treading in their dung we progressed through a maze of cobbled alleyways at quite a pace. We stopped in a small square in which the only other occupants appeared to be three old ladies clad in black, sitting on upturned orange boxes; they ignored us. The boy dived into a miserable looking taverna and soon reappeared with a skinny gaunt very old man who stood unsteadily gawping at Sid with watery blue eyes. The boy handed Sid's trousers to the old man. By this time we had realized he was quite drunk. Sid snatched the pants back from the old man and placed them in front of him to illustrate their enormous girth. The old man swayed, muttered something incoherent and wobbled back to the pub, leaving an infuriated Sid still holding the pants. The boy vanished almost as mysteriously as he had appeared. Although it took us nearly an hour to find our way back to the villa we did stumble across a bakery where Sid was able to appease his wrath by way of a bun feast.

The following day, our last on the island, Sid decided to try a final onslaught against Papandreas to get at least half his money back. After several visits at half hour intervals he was unable to rouse a sign of life from the establishment.

It was months before I dared asked Sid about the fate of his trousers. He told me he was renting them to Lou Costello for his next movie.

Chapter 12

Occasionally Sid would accept an invitation to be a guest lecturer. During the same year as our Greek escapade he spent a month in California as Regent's Lecturer at the University of California Santa Barbara, where he was quartered in a local hotel. Out of sheer boredom, and at someone else's expense, I suspect, he called me in London. He had in deference of his age been placed with a couple of dozen senior citizens. Their average age he guessed to be eighty-five. Some form of gruel was served nightly from five fifteen to six thirty, allowing the inhabitants to watch such power-packed TV spectaculars as the Mary Tyler Moore Show before snuggling down with their mugs of cocoa. Definitely not Sid's nirvana, especially the food which was sneeringly described by him as health food.

'What I would give to drown my sorrows in a bowl of *Lockshen* soup and fondle a bosom or two,' were his parting words.

Following this segment he took part in a BBC programme shot in America, on American humour featuring Woody Allen and other doyens of the New York school.

Pretty soon the mildewed porter at Browns was again putting hot coals in the bed warmer to air Mr Perelman's bed.

Sid and I had always promised ourselves a motor tour of Britain (or at least part of it). So when Sid arrived during a decent weather spell I was inspired to plan a route.

Although he was something of a car enthusiast his enthusiasm did not stretch to being piloted by me at high speed in a Porsche. Therefore he was relieved to find I had acquired a little Alfa Sud, an Italian charmer of more modest performance, but which gave me as much driving pleasure and Sid more room to manoeuvre. We made a beeline for my favourite land, Wales.

Adhering to my pact to drive within the legal speed limit we arrived in time to eat lunch at Bath. This staggeringly beautiful eighteenth century Nash-designed town is arguably the most attractive in Britain. Sid was impressed with its elegance and leisurely pace. We spent an hour inspecting the original Roman bath and spa, and mooching around the lofty assembly rooms. In James Fitzpatrick monotones Sid extolled Bath's virtues as we continued our way to Ross-on-Wye, an ancient Herefordshire county town divided from Wales by the wild and tortuous River Wye.

Close by in an idyllic spot on the side of the hill, lives my good friend American artist, Leonard Creo with his Welsh wife Gillian and their three daughters. He has developed the land surrounding their house into a veritable market garden enabling them to live virtually off their own patch. As a successful respected professional artist Creo has been able to combine his love of nature and art to provide sustenance for a contented family. I was a regular visitor to this haven and Sid had been with me on previous occasions. So it was a jolly reunion and the delicious smells of Gillian's cooking that awaited us.

Creo is a profound man with a highly developed sense of the ridiculous, hence his rapport with Sid. We had arranged to sleep at a local inn alongside the ancient Goodrich Castle. So, filled with food, conversation, and a few glasses of Creo's home-made cider accompanied by jazz tapes, we drove around to where our host was waiting to remove our bags from the car and carry them to our room. By the time Sid had returned the from the 'john' I was tucked up in bed awaiting the sandman.

Sid, however, a creature of habit, was just about to embark on his nightly routine which was like part of a Japanese ceremony. He would carefully fold and hang his clothes on a clothes-hanger, putting them in the closet. He would lay out on the bed his robe and pyjamas, and remove his leather slippers from their case. The ceremony of positioning his antique Gillette razor, brush and soap, was followed by a noisy, but thorough teeth cleaning and gargling session. He would then remove a novel from his case and change over to his reading spectacles. Whilst clearing his throat several times he would climb into bed, after adjusting the reading lamp. Opening the book he would read about one sentence and suddenly nod off. Perhaps an hour or two later he would awaken, place his spectacles and book on the bedside table and go back to sleep.

On this particular warm night the ceremony was interrupted during an early stage before I had quite fallen asleep. I heard the pulling of a zip-fastener, then a gasp and cry.

'The bastards, they've done the old switch.'

Pushing back the sheets from my face I saw Sid with an open British Airways flight bag on his bed and holding in one hand an adjustable wrench, in the other an oily rag. Initially he was not pleased with my response of uncontrollable mirth.

'What the hell's so funny?' he asked after a few moments.

'Sid,' I choked, 'you've got my car toolbag.'

'What do you mean?' he asked.

'Look,' I said, 'your overnight kit is in a British Airways bag which is exactly the same as the one I carry my tools in, obviously in the dark the landlord selected the wrong bag.'

He appreciated the joke as much as I did and as he was still fully dressed volunteered to remedy the situation himself. By the time he had returned from the car with his own bag I had chuckled myself to sleep.

At the Rolls Memorium, Monmouth.

Due to a set of inexplicable circumstances an occasional combination of human beings attract a certain type of happenings. It seems that after so many close encounters of a *meshugge* kind Sid and I had developed a personal ESP wavelength which guided us into these absurd situations.

Meanwhile, after planting the infamous toolbag out of sight, our intrepid heroes once again hit the road to Monmouth. On the fringe of the majestic Black Mountains this little Welsh town is famous as the birthplace of the honourable Charles Stuart Rolls (1877–1910), the salesman part of the renowned motoring partnership. In the travel brochure tradition Sid was photographed by me, standing alongside the Rolls Art Nouveau memorial statue. Following a trail of minor minor-mountain roads, barely wide enough for my small car and often blocked by sheep, we managed in a forward and backward process to negotiate our way through to the spectacular eleventh century Llantony Abbey. This desolate, ghostly looking ruin surrounded by the Black Mountains was as appropriate a setting for the antics of Bela Lugosi as anything conjured up on the RKO backlot. Somehow an enterprising Victoria gentleman had salvaged a relatively watertight portion of the ruins and converted them into a kind of pub guest house. The entire effect was more reminiscent of Queen Elizabeth the First, not the Second. The charming and apologetic proprietor told us that the only available room was somewhat primitive but appropriately inexpensive. To the very top of an eerie stone tower we climbed up what seemed like hundreds of well-worn steps of a narrow spiral staircase, then collapsed on to a couple of lumpy beds before surveying our surroundings. On inspection the room looked like the last resting place of St Jerome the hermit. Running water would have been a space-age luxury, there was just a jug and basin on top of an iron Victorian washstand. A huge oak wardrobe covered about fifty per cent of the floor space. How on earth they got it up there I can't imagine. As the construction of the pyramids is one of the great mysteries of ancient Egypt, this must be one of the great mysteries of ancient Wales. The tiny window, after much muscular persuasion from both Sid and me, remained stubbornly shut. There was at least one feeble light dangling in a flyblown shade from the centre of the room.

'Last in bed puts the light out,' I said to Sid. He grimaced.

76

'And don't trip over the chamber pot,' I added.

Under the circumstances our efforts to clean up were none too successful but hardened travellers as we were we made it down to the communal dining room. Low, and full of magnificent early Welsh oak furniture, I was in clover. Sid and I sat with a group of eight people at a fine baronial table. The food was super home-made country fare, well cooked and seasoned. Sid obviously approved, tucking in heartily. The other diners were English tourists displaying their native reserve by politely ignoring us and chatting amongst themselves. We eavesdropped on a section of their conversation, listening to a gentleman informing two awestruck middle-aged ladies that the East Tower had the reputation of being haunted by a figure in white appearing from time to time on the staircase. I looked at Sid whose face remained inscrutable but whom I could almost hear chuckling inwardly. After a couple of beers in the dingy pub hollowed out from a medieval dungeon. We trudged up the staircase to our room. Of course I was in bed like a shot and noticed that Sid had decided to curtail his nightly ritual somewhat as his bedsprings were groaning within a few moments. I must have slumbered soundly for a few hours as when I awoke I noticed the dawn light filtering through the muck-encrusted window panes. As I lay there I became aware that I had been awoken by a persistent rustling and tapping noise somewhere close by. As it persisted I became more and more curious, then hearing Sid's bed groan I whispered to him,

'Can you hear a weird noise?'

'Yes, what is it?' he whispered back. We strained our ears to listen to the persistent rustling. 'Sounds like something on the staircase,' hissed Sid.

'I thought you'd say that,' I replied, adding, 'and I suppose you want me to take the torch and investigate?'

'Why?' he asked. 'Are you scared?'

Pulling on my socks and pants I crept towards the door, clutching my torch. Fearing that the ancient hinges would squeak loudly I opened it very cautiously, the noises without were definitely coming from the spiral staircase, I turned back towards Sid who was now sitting up in bed.

'Well go on,' he prodded.

As stealthily as possible I tip-toed down the stairs. The

noises persisted and seemed to be accompanied by clucking sounds. Around the next spiral was an open stone apperture over which someone had placed a kind of sack-covered frame. In this framework now sat two large white ducks, flapping their wings and somehow clicking their bills against the stonework. As I shone the torch directly at them they took off, no doubt for the pond below. Sid was by this time peering nervously around the door tying his bathrobe.

To my earthly explanation of these ghostly manifestations Sid's reply was, 'Well now I'm up I am bursting for a pee. Where do I go?'

'Me too,' I replied, dragging the chamber pot from beneath the bed. During the next half hour I heard muted chuckles coming from Sid's bed.

Whilst eating our breakfast at the long table we were gradually joined by the 'Whodunnit' group, each one mumbling, 'Good morning,' as they seated themselves. This monastic, but satisfying meal was abruptly interrupted by Sid.

'Pardon me,' he said to the assembled, but I could not help overhearing your conversation during last evening's meal when you discussed supernatural happenings in the East Tower.' All eyes were on him as he continued, 'My companion and I spent the night in the tower room'. Sid's immaculate timing then came into play, as he poured himself another coffee and took a leisurely sip, showing no interest in elaborating on his previous statement.

The gaunt middle-aged gent, sporting a bow tie, opposite Sid succumbed to his curiosity by piping, 'I say, did anything strange happen during the night?'

Sid slowly looked up from his coffee cup.

'Yes,' he replied, rising to leave the room, 'At dawn we found two ducks on the staircase, good morning.'

From the 'haunted' abbey we drove on through wild moorland and spectacular scenery to the small town of Hay-on-Wye. One of the highlights of our tour. This remote town is regarded as the book centre of Britain. I was acquainted with the charming eccentric who had started the metamorphosis from sleepy town to bustling book centre about fifteen years previously. He is Richard Booth who then resided in a dilapidated local castle and had proclaimed himself the King of Hay. This dedicated bibliophile was a rare combination of businessman, scholar and humorist. He had chosen Hay because of its beauty, compactness, and geographical situation close to the centre of Britain. Starting with the tiny local bookshop he had gradually bought out several other small shops and filled them with books of all types, new, secondhand, and ancient. On hearing that the local cinema was about to present its 'Last Picture Show', he made a bid and filled it with thousands of books. Later on he even acquired the fire station* (and also filled it with books) and a couple of warehouses for good measure. Millions and millions of books.

Sid was in his element as we meandered between the shelves and stacks in the cinema awaiting an audience with 'His Majesty'. Richard Booth, of course, was well acquainted with Sid's work and delighted to meet him. He gave us tea and a grand tour of his rambling kingdom. Whilst in one of the warehouses I chanced to pick out of a box an out-of-print volume about the actress, Patricia Neal, and husband writer, Roald Dahl, both known by Sid and myself. So when we called to see them at the end of our trip we had the ideal gift. After several fascinating hours with Richard we continued to our day's destination. The perfectly preserved sixteenth century walled Shropshire town of Ludlow.

We checked into the ancient and aristocratic Feather's Hotel and after enjoying the very English roast beef dinner, retired to the luxury of our separate rooms. Sid was entranced with the old town. We visited the tiny museum and later strolled around admiring the lovely black and white timber buildings. In fact Sid got so enthusiastic that he stopped at each estate agent's shop to enquire about the price of local cottages. After a cheesy lunch in an old ladies tea room we drove on, recrossing the border into Wales. Welsh place names are almost unpronounceable to anyone but the Welsh speaking inhabitants. To Sid they were a challenge, one special tongue twister, he noticed, was Llanfyllin out of which came his classic distortion 'Llaintfyllin'.†

---

* I never did enquire what had happened to the fire brigade but significantly some time after our visit a major part of his castle was destroyed by fire.

There are many beautiful areas in Britain and touring the remote parts can be very rewarding. My own particular favourite spot is the Snowdonia Park which covers a large portion of North Wales. Dominated by the Snowdonia Mountain range and punctuated by several lakes including the magnificent duo, Bala and Vyrnny. This sparcely populated country with its uncluttered roads and awesome beauty makes motoring the joy it was way back. Sid soaked up this marvellous scenery on the way to our next destination, the tiny but famous village of Portmeirion.

In Portmeirion.

Portmeirion is situated overlooking Tremadoc Bay in the Welsh county of Merioneth. It has a delightful facade which was gradually built between the wars by another eccentric in the Richard Booth mould, a Welsh architect named Clough Williams-Ellis, now a nonagenarian, he had acquired Aberia, as the peninsula was then known, from an old lady recluse in

---

† Any eagle-eyed Hebrew scholar who might be reading this will immediately identify the name as 'Laying *Tfillin*' — meaning the daily ceremony of donning the sacred straps and boxes containing miniature scrolls of the law.

the early 1920s. He was a man who hated to see anything go to waste so accumulated all the interesting facias of buildings which were about to be torn down. The style or period of architecture was unimportant, the aesthetic quality was. This fantastic collection of giant bric-a-brac included monuments, archways, pedestals, and portals from all over Britain which had been erected during the last three centuries or so. Although Ellis built these original columns and facias into his dream project, the private village, which he named Portmeirion, was referred to by him as this home for fallen buildings.

What an incredible mixture of Hansel and Gretel, Ruritania and Walt Disney it had developed into. One enters the estate along a tree-lined road and parks outside the actual entrance lodge, a little man pops out and collects a quid and you enter into this Welsh Shangrila. Sid viewed it with disbelief. The buildings and fountains and shops are all painted in fairyland colours and one expects Rumplestiltskin to pop up under your nose any moment. It even has a hotel* where we took a room overlooking the fine white beach and clear water of the bay. Rinky-tinky as the village is, the hotel definitely is not. *Chichi*, cozy, costly would be my 'three little words' but our overnight stay was enjoyable.

My home territory is Lancashire in the north-west of England. Although I was born and raised in Manchester my family moved to Southport during the early war years and have remained there ever since (minus me of course). So, leaving Portmerion we headed for the Roman city of Deva (let's call it Chester), en route for Southport. Chester with its fine, well preserved Tudor and Elizabethan arcades raised above street level was a childhood venue of mine. Dad would drive us there in the Chrysler for Sunday afternoon tea. Sid appreciated our whirlwind tour of the city.

On through the Mersey Tunnel and the depressing city suburbs of Liverpool, which were not improved by the still oppressive heat and humidity. Most people associate Liverpool with The Beatles and it therefore has an aura of glamour in their minds. Those that do make the pilgrimage

* Unfortunately damaged by fire quite recently but about to be rebuilt. Any connection with Booth's castle fire purely coincidental.

come down to earth with a bump. Liverpool looks like the thirties depression is still going strong. Miles of decayed and vandalized commercial properties, throngs of out-of-work people hanging around outside the multitude of pubs, and graffiti everywhere. It is hard to believe that this city has cradled several of Britain's top entertainers.

Southport, although only eighteen miles from Liverpool, is as different as Beverly Hills is from Bayonne, New Jersey. A Victorian seaside town of elegance and style it boasts of one of Britain's loveliest main streets, Lord Street, a huge beach area and typical nineteenth century pier and promenade. My mother's handsome, modern bungalow is situated opposite one of the world's greatest golf courses (so they tell me, I never touch 'em myself), the Royal Birkdale.

My family, comprising my mother, sister Sybil, husband Cyril and teenagers Michael and Jane were waiting *en masse* to greet us. Even as we drove up the driveway Sid's nose began to twitch significantly as the delicious odour of *blintzes* cooking reached it. Every son swears his mum is the best cook, well in this instance I will stand by tradition. My own mum is by no stretch of the imagination a *Yiddisher Mama*, she is stylish, attractive, and has a lively sense of humour. Occasionally though, for appreciative family visitors such as myself she will 'Let her hair down' and prepare a *kosher* feast.

Although none of the family actually knew who S. J. Perelman was, my description of him as a famous Jewish American author and close friend was enough to stimulate their interest and ensure a very warm welcome. Sybil's bubbling personality and skill as a hilarious raconteur quickly endeared her to Sid as she plied him with chopped liver on *matzoh*. The reverberations of my mother's chopping could still be heard from the kitchen. Cyril was explaining to me over a sherry that he was awaiting a call confirming the sale of his boat and also a guy was expected that evening to look over Sybil's car which was also for sale. Jane and Michael appeared carrying steaming bowls of chicken soup as we all sat down at the table. Sid was in his element declaring that not for many years had he enjoyed a real home-made meal so much.

During the meal the 'phone rang twice, both times Cyril shot up to answer it and quickly returned telling Sybil it was either the boat man or the car man and that they would call back after dinner. Fortunately nothing was spilt over Sid's trousers nor were we disturbed again until after the meal when we had settled down in comfortable chairs to drink coffee and *schmooze*.

Within moments the door bell rang which in turned caused Oscar, the Scottie, to streak, yapping from the kitchen to the front door. Jane who was sitting next to Sid sprang up to open the door causing the sugar basin, resting on the arm of Sid's chair, to empty its contents over Sid's pants. Sid rose sharply in a shower of sugar, Jane apologetically started to brush him off with a serviette and momentarily everyone, despite Oscar's continued yapping, forgot about the front door. When it rang for the second time I opened it up to find a small lady standing outside. She explained to me that she was Mrs So-and-so who had arranged to meet her husband here and look at a car which had been offered for sale in the local paper. Cyril had come forward by this time and was smilingly explaining to the lady that he was expecting her husband to 'phone him at any moment.

'Oh,' she replied, 'he told me he would be here at seven thirty. So I came by straight after seeing my mother in hospital.'

'Well,' said Cyril, 'you'd better come in and have a cup of coffee, I am sure you won't be waiting for long.'

As he ushered her into the living room Sybil was vacuuming around Sid's chair whilst Jane was still brushing him down. Through the din of the vacuum cleaner the 'phone could be heard ringing.

'Shut up!' shouted Cyril as he lifted the 'phone. Then he turned to the lady who appeared to be hiding behind a curtain to assure her that her husband would be around in five minutes. For about two or three of the five minutes things were fairly normal, just another 'phone call which Sybil answered this time. She turned to Cyril, with her hand over the 'phone mouthpiece.

'I think it's the guy about the boat,' she said, 'not the one that called earlier, the dealer from last week.'

'How did he get my number here?' asked Cyril.

'Don't you remember you told him to try here if there was no reply at our house,' she replied. Cyril nodded as he picked up the 'phone, after a cryptic series of 'yeses' and 'nos' the conversation terminated.

'I'll call you back later.' Cyril smiled and groaned simultaneously, 'This fellow thinks he's got a punter for the boat for the original asking price, and now I've almost done a deal with the other guy for less money!'

The volume of the latter half of Cyril's statement tailed off as he realized that the little lady was still shyly standing partially hidden behind the curtain. Not for long, however, as the door bell rang again, it was a race between Oscar and Cyril as to who reached it first but Cyril definitely opened it. At that precise moment Sybil picked up the ringing 'phone, Cyril was greeting the lady's husband when Sybil called him. Immediately the little lady had recognized her husband's voice she scurried towards the door and his protection, passing en route Cyril who had excused himself momentarily to attend Sybil's bidding. She told him it was the other man about the boat.

'Which one?' queried Cyril.

'The one who rang earlier,' whispered Sybil, adding 'You had better talk to him now as he says he has to go out fairly soon.'

'Then you had better demonstrate the car,' replied Cyril. 'I can't do two things at once.' Sybil protested that she couldn't demonstrate cars.

'Well, what can I do?' Cyril shrugged as he picked up the 'phone. Sybil turned around to Michael who was attempting to participate in a normal conversation with his Grandma and Sid.

'Look,' she said to him as she fished the car keys from her handbag, 'take these and show the lady and gentleman my car.'

As Michael resignedly agreed to demonstrate the car, I happened to glance at Sid. His outward calm expression did not betray what I guessed to be his inward hysterics at the scene unfolding around him. Or maybe it was the three large chocolates he had accepted in quick succession from the box proffered by my mum that had prevented him from betraying his true feelings. Cyril returned from the 'phone to seek Sybil's and my opinion on the best solution to his dilemma: whether he should accept the offer of more money from an unknown dealer or stick to his own offer of a bargain price to an acquaintance. Everyone jumped when the door bell rang again. It couldn't be Michael returning as the door was open and he would have walked in. This time my mother called out, 'Who is it?'

In a rich Lancashire accent a voice replied, 'It's me Madam, Mr Rimmer, I've come to measure the kitchen floor.'

My mother looked perplexed as she replied, 'Oh you'd better come in Mr Rimmer, I am sorry I had forgotten our appointment'.

As the old chap made his way to the kitchen my mother explained to Sid that Mr Rimmer was a local handyman whom she had engaged to lay down new floor tiles.

The final outcome of all this evening's activity remained a mystery to me, as Sybil, Cyril and family went home shortly afterwards, hopefully to conclude a successful evening's business. Leaving mum who is a grand sport to enjoy a good laugh about it all with Sid and me. In fact Sid even played his part in the evening's varied transactions. On opening a wardrobe in his bedroom he spotted a fine heavy sheepskin coat hanging there. Before leaving the next morning he asked Mum about it, adding it was just what he needed to combat the New York winters. She told him her late husband (another Sydney) had had it specially made for him in Austria but had rarely worn it. Sid asked if he could try on the coat and its matching fur hat. It was a perfect fit and a price was agreed. So at least one successful transaction was completed.

After leaving, and as we drove to nearby Blackpool, Sid commented that our stay was definitely an all-*kosher* version of Noel Coward's *Hay Fever*.

On the other side of the Fylde coast bay, and in complete contrast to quiet residential Southport lies the heart of northern fun-and-frolics, Blackpool. This Victorian counterpart of Atlantic City, Coney Island, Las Vegas and Disney Land rolled into one, is Britain's most famous seaside town. Dominated by the Blackpool Tower, a similar and rival structure to the Eiffel Tower, it was the first major purpose-built pleasure resort. Anyone who was raised in the north of England has happy memories about Blackpool, its beaches, the tower, the gigantic pleasure grounds. Its famous Golden Mile, with novelty sideshows, its beach, donkeys, piers, tram cars, spectacular illuminations, and all the rest of the paraphernalia which contributed to mass 'fun'.

As guests of the Blackpool publicity department, Sid and I were given the Royal treatment, a whistle stop tour of life's pleasures. To me pure dribbling nostalgia, to Sid a real eye-opener. We were even shown over the superb Victorian gilded Opera house, The Winter Gardens, and gigantic Tower Ballroom. We lunched on the local delicacy of fresh fish and chips and generally plunged into the effervescent festive atmosphere. We took sherry with Blackpool's Lord Mayor who had no doubt been briefed on Sid's background.

At . . . (Loggerheads).

'Well, well,' he said on meeting him, 'I've always wanted to shake the hand of the man who wrote for the Marx Brothers.'

Officialdom could not have been more charming, providing us with rooms in their finest hotel, The Metropole, plus a slap-up dinner and bedtime reading in the form of books of facts, figures and history of the town. Sid enjoyed reading about some of the legendary northern entertainers who had played the pier theatres: George Formby, Ted Ray, Stanley Holloway, Sir Harry Lauder, Will Hay and many more.

Early the next day we crossed the spectacular Pennine Range, and through the black witch country, dividing Lancashire and Yorkshire. We lunched in York, almost a northern equivalent of Bath in its splendour, but of a much earlier architectural style and popped into the marvellous York Museum which, to do it justice, requires at least a day's inspection. I did manage to show Sid the best bits though. Entire eighteenth century shopping streets with original mullioned-window shop-fronts, interiors and goods on display.

Driving south from there, passing through my home town, Manchester, we passed the dark satanic mills of Stockport and Staley Bridge, heading for a remote spot in the centre of the Derbyshire Dales, where Tony and Ruth Wright, old Mancunian friends of mine, had arranged to accommodate us for the night. What I did not expect was the surprise party given in our honour and comprising several old northern friends of mine whom I had not seen in years. A warm and wonderful evening.

We drove through the potteries. The Staffordshire centre for pottery and porcelain for hundreds of years. Home of Wedgewood, Doulton, Pratt wear and other manufacturers whose names are part of English history. After dropping in for tea with the Dahls at their Buckinghamshire home, we made it back to London in time for dinner. Sid's elation was obvious. A week of insane incidents with a background of beautiful Britain, was definitely his glass of tea.

Chapter 13

At least once a year Sid would call on his old Hollywood buddy, screen writer Donald Ogden Stewart. Stewart had lived for many years in an historic rambling Hampstead house with his wife Ella Winters, a lady of strong character and determination and whose political views did not correspond with her lifestyle. Surrounded by oriental antiques and twentieth century art their house with its patina of faded luxury had a museum-like atmosphere in which Ella acted as the curator rather than hostess.

As an aficionado of primitive and ethnic art Ella frequently appeared in the Portal Gallery. Where she regularly purchased one or more paintings. Just as regularly she returned them a few days later. A kind of game I resignedly agreed to play in admiration for her sheer *chutzpah*. Husband Don on the other hand was in complete contrast a gentle, quiet and wickedly witty man. He was greatly admired by many.

Two or three times a year I would visit them with either Sid or Max and Barbara Wilk. The usual event being a weekend tea party. On this particular visit besides Sid and myself were the writer John Collier and his wife and a few other close friends of Don and Ella.

The old house was built on split levels, its long narrow living room led out on to a pleasant garden. Down the centre of the living room sat a long low table cluttered with antique knick-knacks, a samovar, a Chinese tea set and for this particular occasion a large yummy looking iced walnut cake. During the course of Don's amusing introductions to those few of us who did not know each other there was a sudden shriek from Ella who had been fussing about with paper napkins and teaspoons.

'Don, Don,' she wailed, 'it's the black dog, get it out, it will jump on Fi-Fi.'*

* The little bitch's real name has been changed to save any unnecessary distress to her family.

88

Followed by a trail of napkins and all our eyes she stumbled through the open French windows into the garden where tiny Fi-Fi, trailing a long leather lead, was being pursued by a large black dog which had appeared from nowhere via a fence. Don with all the alacrity an octogenerian could muster, restrained the screaming Ella and somehow managed to put his foot on Fi-Fi's lead. Sid and I were just about able to stop him from falling as we grabbed the lead. Meanwhile, our fellow guests had 'shooed' the black dog out of the garden and were consoling the semi-hysterical Ella who insisted in safely locking the on-heat Fi-Fi in the downstairs kitchen.

We returned to a relatively calm living room and after a while Ella announced that she would go down to prepare tea. The ladies present volunteered to assist but these offers she firmly declined. Despite her severe arthritis and generally delicate health Ella still dressed in the ethnic hippy style, and make-up of the mid-sixties, wearing floor length Indian dresses encrusted with brightly coloured stones and braid, her bosom was adorned with strings of beads and massive silver necklaces. How should could move at all when she must have been wearing at least five pounds in weight of silver bracelets and bangles on each arm was a mystery to me.

She slowly hauled herself out of the room and we heard her clanking ghost-like down the stairs towards the kitchen. Suddenly the sounds of a pogrom erupted from below, piercing shrieks from Ella, accompanied by great crashes. Everyone in the room rushed for the stairs together leaving a doddering Don in our wake. All six of us burst into the kitchen to find water cascading from a full sink, where a totally hysterical Ella was attempting to heave up a zinc bucket, like Liza at the well. On the stone floor was an assortment of spades, shovels and domestic appliances. For a few moments the scene was totally incomprehensible and Ella was quite unable to explain. It was only when a canine wimper drew our attention to Fi-Fi that we began to get the picture. Her dripping head and front paws were protruding through the small dog-flap at the bottom of the kitchen door, whilst her rear end had been mounted by the growling black dog on the outside, they were locked in sexual union.

Poor Ella had been filling the tea kettle when she realized what was happening and immediately panicked. Grabbing a bucket she poured the water from the kettle into it and tipped it over Fi-Fi and her mate, then grabbed a shovel and banged it on the door whilst shrieking at the black dog. Ella's hysteria must have contributed to her enormous burst of speed and energy as all this hullabaloo had occurred within minutes. We managed to restrain her physical efforts but not her shrieks or sobs.

'Get them apart! He will kill Fi-Fi!'

Sid stared incredulously at the scene, then suggested that it was dangerous and harmful to interfere with coupled dogs. Our first action was obviously to get the protesting Ella out of the way as she was still attempting to empty a bucket of water over the poor animals. The ladies eventually got her out of the kitchen and into her bedroom. We turned off the water and cleaned up the mess, under Don's calm supervision. He seemed to be quite used to Ella's outbursts over the black dog. Meanwhile the rather pathetic animals continued their jig until suddenly with a little moan they parted. As this juncture a young lady obviously *au fait* with the shenannigans of the Ogden Stewart household, mysteriously appeared to take charge. We were all asked to return to the living room where tea would be served promptly.

As Sid and I tucked into the walnut cake the scene was re-enacted with great glee by all of us. The three writers present agreed on *Dog Day Afternoon* as the title for the play. After a while a somewhat subdued Ella entered the room cradling a still damp Fi-Fi in her arms. She announced that she had managed to locate a veterinary emergency service who had agreed to treat Fi-Fi for any possible consequence that might have occurred during coitus. A ring at the door announced the arrival of a taxi to take Ella and Fi-Fi and the mysterious lady to the clinic. When Don returned from escorting Ella to the taxi he grinned at Sid and I whilst fishing out a bottle of Scotch from behind the bookcase.

Sid had been bitten by the 'Ludlow bug', expressing a desire to return there and buy an old cottage. He would not be fobbed off with my reasoning that it was an impractical idea. He just loved the place and insisted on going back for another *shufti* before his return to New York. I drove him down to Creo's with whom he stayed for a few days whilst exploring the local countryside by bus. Although his enthusiasm for

Ludlow did not diminish after a second look he did realize that geographically it was rather a remote place to be settled in without local friends, and with not even a whiff of salt-beef for at least a hundred miles.

On our return to London we stopped off at the incongruously situated museum of Imperialist White Russia. This now defunct 'side-show' suddenly popped up from behind a hedge near Llandogo. Comprising a few rooms situated over an undistinguished village shop, it is presided over by a self-styled White Russian Count. This nobleman obviously slept late as, although it was 1 pm, we had quite a job arousing him and his mangy Borzoi. Eventually, after heaving on a cable-operated bell several times, the door opened a crack to reveal a tall bearded man wearing a huge astrakhan hat and Cossack costume.

The fact that he looked at least forty years younger than he should have done, if he had been a White Russian, didn't deter us. I figured his youthfulness could be attributed to a diet of *Azerbaijam* yoghurt. In a bass voice with a stage Russian accent he enquired what we wanted. When we pointed to the hand-written sign on the door declaring the museum to be open daily from 10 am to 5 pm, he nodded, introduced himself and demanded one pound from each of us. On receiving his fee he called the aged Borzoi to heel and motioned for us to follow him up the dingy staircase.

The collection of phoney relics hanging on the walls and on display in the dusty, wobbly showcases came straight out of an amateur theatrical society cast-off chest. Amongst the 'priceless' mementoes he pointed at were an old shoe supposedly belonging to the real Anastasia, a cracked lorgnette, the alleged property of Czar Nicholas's Mama and a collection of 'highly important' and completely undecipherable rat-eaten documents proving his own heritage. The premises stank of dog excreta which I am certain even assailed the nostrils of our noble host. He would pause mid-sentence, sniff, then begin furiously puffing smoke from his foot-long cheroot into the darkest corners of the museum cum mausoleum.

When this nightmare mini-tour of White Russia was over we speedily returned to the land of the living. Very much so in fact, as that evening we ate and listened to the great Count Basie Band at Ronnie Scott's club as the guests of Walter Houser.*

'Two phoney Counts in one day,' remarked Sid as we left the club. 'It's gotta be a record.'

Shortly after Sid's return to New York he sent a distinguished emissary to visit me. I was flattered when an elegant lady walked into the gallery one day and introduced herself as Lillian Hellman. An old and close friend of Sid's and one of America's foremost authors I was intrigued to meet her. We arranged a Saturday lunch at Langan's Brasserie, the excellent ever-popular London restaurant where I just happen to play with my jazz group most evenings. As we entered the restaurant together Lillian Hellman's presence was noticed by a group of well-known American movie people lunching at the top table and there was a break in the conversation as we passed by. Lillian ignored their stares as she sat down at a nearby centre table opposite me and with her back towards them.

People like Lillian Hellman are rare, she has that special ability to fulfil her role as author into her private life. The intensity, dignity and humour of her works spill over into her conversation. Besides our mutual affection for Sid and his fads and fancies, we covered common ground, comparing life in London and New York. I appreciated Lillian's pungent humour and satirical comments on both places. To me a most pleasurable interlude.

Before ordering our meal I had noticed two of the movie moguls still gazing in our direction. One of them was obviously telling his companion my name. Although, through the gallery I was acquainted with most of the people seated at the table, I guess I was generally known as 'small fry' within their circle. So when I walked in the place with such a respected celebrity's celebrity as Lillian Hellman, it must have irritated them not to have remembered my name. On leaving, however, the situation changed. I was escorting Lillian towards the wreath of havanna cigar smoke encircling their

---

* Walter claims to have the distinction of being the only member of our 'group' to have been treated by Sid to a 'full works' dinner in an expensive restaurant.

92

table when two or three of them waved and beckoned to me.

'Hi.'

'Hello Eric. How are you.'

Somewhat surprised at their sudden sociability I asked Lillian (who knew who all of them were) if she would care to stop at the table.

'Screw 'em', she murmured, winking at me as we walked out.

Chapter 14

The first inkling of 'things to come' was a call from Sid early in 1978. We regularly carried on a crisp correspondence about all our activities. This was topped up with an occasional 'phone call when one of us had something urgent to say, as both of us believed in value for money we skipped the formalities and talked fast. Sid told me he had kicked around an idea with Harry Evans, editor of the London *Sunday Times*, over dinner in New York. Through the years Sid had often sought my opinion as to the current value of his MG which was still in 'mothballs', residing in Bucks County. We had discussed various schemes of shipping it over to Europe where we would use it for a grand tour of Ireland or even the continent. Alternatively, as the car increased in value Sid rubbed his hands more briskly and talked of selling. However, when it came to the crunch Sid's nostalgic side overcame his mercenary one and the little MG still remained his property after almost thirty years.

Initially Sid's conversation sounded too fantastic to be practical. He and Harry thought it would be possible for Sid and another party to retrace the route of the Peking to Paris Motor Race of 1907 in the MG.

'Of course,' he added, 'the route would be reversed, starting from Paris covering as much of the original as possible and it would not be a race, just a solo drive.'

'Sid,' I bellowed, 'you must be joking, to cover eight or nine thousand miles in a thirty-year-old car. Do you realize how tough it would be?' I then reminded him of my hair-raising drive to India in 1966.

'Sure, sure,' said Sid. 'But is it possible?'

I paused (despite his 'phone bill), 'Possible yes. Practical, no.'

'To hell with *practical*,' Sid chimed in. 'If I can work you into the deal are you game?'

'Sid,' I replied, 'to me it's the one I've been waiting for.'

'OK,' replied Sid. 'Write me your own ideas on such a trip and see what information you can find about the original race.'

At that he rung off, leaving my imagination boggling. Based very loosely on the Peking–Paris race, the successful comedy movie, *The Great Race*, featuring Tony Curtis and Terry Thomas is as much as the public remembers about the event. Unless, of course, they happen to be ninety-three-year-old motor racing buffs. There have been several books on the event over the years, the most famous being *Peking to Paris*, an account written by Luigi Barzini (Junior), son of Luigi Barzini the Italian Journalist who was a member of Prince Borghese's winning crew in an Itala motor car. Another excellent book on the subject, *The Mad Motorists*, was written by Alan Andrews in 1964. It was a copy of this latter version, now out of print and difficult to come by, that I forwarded to Sid with a letter full of suggestions as to the format of the trip. Within a short time our transatlantic lines were buzzing and our mail boxes brimming with plans.

The finally agreed format between Sid and Harry Evans was that *The Sunday Times* was to sponsor an expedition. This comprised Sid and a young popsie of his choice in the MG leading myself and a mechanic in a heavily laden back-up Range Rover. Sid was to send a series of reports to *The Sunday Times* at specific intervals en route. Despite the fact that there were still several months to go before D-day (planned for September 1st) we entered into the preparations with great gusto.

The Sunday Times contacted a veteran MG expert named Sid Beer.* This worthy gentleman owns a well-established family MG car business and fine collection of early MGs in Huntingdon. He agreed that when the car arrived (it was by this time crated and en route by sea) he would check it over and make any necessary modifications. He also agreed to act as co-driver with me in the Rover, and of course, to be the expedition's mechanic.

On the due date the MG arrived and I was impressed. Finished in original black with its separate fenders and chromium headlamps, and its tan pigskin upholstery, it took me right back to the same four-seat model (the only difference

---

* To avoid confusion with the first Sid I shall refer henceforth to the second one by his surname.

was that ours was a sedan version) owned by my father in 1952. As I slid into the bucket seat and started it up to drive it to *The Sunday Times* garage waves of nostalgic MG Magic swept over me. The same direct steering, crisp gearbox, gutsy little motor and rock hard ride as I remembered from a bygone era. Later that day I handed over the keys to Beer who drove it away for its rejuvenation.*

Sid, during the interim period, had managed to cope with the difficult task of selecting his young lady co-driver. He called me to extol her virtues which he assured me were all in the right places, the thought of their close proximity to him in the cockpit of a small MG sports car was already causing him sleepless nights.

'Oh, by the way,' he added, 'I will be over next week to work on the detail planning with you.'

His campaign headquarters was the bedroom of a small private hotel in South Kensington, cheaper and more appropriate than the luxury of Browns, and after all it was good practice to start roughing it early on. Firstly, I drove him to the country to meet Beer and view the MG modifications which were already well under way. We spent an interesting hour viewing Beer's important collection of almost every model of MG that had ever left the factory. His wife prepared an excellent lunch for us during which Beer told us of his lifetime's passion for the marque.

On our return to London that evening I was scheduled to play with my jazz group at Langan's Brasserie so Sid accompanied me there to dinner. The founder, Peter Langan, renowned for his restaurant expertise, his unlimited capacity for Champagne and blend of subtle and coarse wit, joined us at the table. During the ensuing verbal duel between Irish banter and New Yorkeese drawl following my description to Peter of our proposed trip, it became very clear that he and Sid did not exactly see eye-to-eye. So when Peter offered a challenge to Sid in the form of a substantial wager that the MG would never make it to China. Sid, who was not usually a betting man, stiffly agreed.†

---

* Actually with only 19,000 miles on the clock the car was in such excellent mechanical condition that it required very few parts. But Beer modified the electrical system and interior.

Between trips to *The Sunday Times* offices to discuss budget matters and the Royal Automobile Club who were arranging our visas and assisting us with the route, we were kept pretty busy. Much midnight oil was burnt by us constantly pouring over lists of the 'necessities' we would be requiring en route. Second only to candy store windows. Sid's nose was trained to press itself against the window of any war-surplus shop that was in the vicinity, so when he had a genuine excuse to mosey around the stores as a potential client he was in clover. Based on fifty years experience as a traveller Sid knew the importance of such items as primus stoves, combination-folding knife, fork and spoon sets, mosquito nets, ice axes (circa 1945), water-purifying tablets, tins of solidified cocoa, blow lamps, string hammocks, string vests, enamel shaving mugs, cut-throat razors and ex-army shaving brushes, bush jackets, white Norwegian silk hats, solar topes, inflatable water wings, bell tents, one gallon stone jars of blue-black ink, protracter sets, to name but a few.

From the yellow pages of London's business 'phone directory we extracted the addresses of all those surplus and camping shops within a ten-mile radius of Kensington. Systematically, we visited them. Armed with our shopping list Sid would invariably plunge into a dingy corner of the store and attempt to reach for something like a khaki felt-covered enamelled water bottle, inconveniently resting on the highest shelf. This rummaging would usually attract the attention of the proprietor or an assistant, who noticing an old gent straining on tip-toe, would bring a step ladder over on which he would retrieve the object. Sid would politely thank him and after scrutinizing the object would hold a mock conference with me before declaring it was too large or small as the case may be. Careful shopper that Sid was he really surpassed himself on these occasions.

After countless fascinating hours spent in these establishments Sid managed to whittle our original list of over thirty essential items down to the three which we actually purchased, a waterproof ground sheet, two pairs of ex-navy mittens, and a keyring with a minute, everlasting flash-lamp attached.

Naturally the supply of spare parts required for the MG was

---

† Despite the obvious sincerity of both parties, in the heat of the moment the wager was never mentioned again.

In the strangest places (Austria).

In the dog-house. Three of us slept in this seven foot by six foot hut in Hungary.

The expedition on the road to Mount Ararat, Armenia.

Outside the Café Diarrhoea, Afghanistan.
En route (London–Peking)

Sid loved this one outside a Pakistani book publishers.

Taj Mahal, India. Well you did tell us to look you up when we were passing (note Sid's carpet bag).

Two minutes later, Sid was splattered in cow dung, as the MG drove on to this ferry in India.

China border. The end of the line after 8,000 miles.

attended to by Beer. I was designated to look after the food supplies. These, I decided must be chosen with their nourishment content in mind rather than their appeal to Sid's sweet tooth. Therefore I concentrated on conveniently packaged health foods like dried fruits, soup cubes, biscuits, a dozen cases of fruit juices and in deference to Sid, several blocks of Bendick's Sporting and Military chocolate.

'I guess there's no such thing as Jewish health foods,' said a somewhat despondent Sid after reading my list of purchases. 'But surely you could include one case of Bloom's *kreplach* or *knedlach* soup.' I assured him I would.

He returned to New York to collect his own kit and of course his delectable companion. Before leaving there were several going away parties to attend and pre-trip publicity items to deal with so Sid was constantly on the go. On the eve of his return to London Sid and his Golden Tootsie were guests of honour at a large party given by a PR company. The guests included a number of people connected with the book world who were known to Sid. It was during a casual conversation with Sid that one of the guests ignited a bombshell. On checking the facts a furious Sid almost cancelled the expedition. Still simmering he called me within an hour of its happening to tell me the news. His innocent 'Rose of Texas', with an obvious eye for a deal had already sold her own story of the trip to a rival source for a tidy fistful of dollars.

Sid could hardly credit her *chutzpah* and when she tearfully admitted her misdemeanour he did not give her a second chance.

'None of her charms can persuade me to reinstate her,' he assured me slowly adding, 'Now what do we do?'

We decided to carry on regardless and play it by ear when he got to London.

Sid was jittery when, heavily laden, he arrived at Heathrow the next day. We headed for South Kensington where we were to hold a top level conference over a bowl of *borscht*. Sid thought that through a few 'phone calls to his English lady friends he would soon discover one who would be delighted to drive an ancient car half way across the world over a period of months and in the company of three men. After twenty-four hours of frantic 'phone calls and consultations with Harry Evans it was decided to take pot luck. An advert was inserted in *The Times* (daily not *Sunday*) for an adventurous female driver willing to accompany a well-known author on a vintage car trip from London to China. The avalanche of replies we expected did not quite materialize. Actually we received four and I was designated to interview the applicants whilst Sid sat by in silent scrutiny. None of these ladies (three actually appeared) came up to Sid's physical standards so we were back to square one with only ten days to 'D-day'.

Beer notified us that the MG was in tip-top condition and ready to go. There was, however, no sign of the back-up Range Rover from Leyland, despite several calls from *The Sunday Times*. It was only when we did receive a letter from them telling us that with regret they had to withdraw their offer of a vehicle due to financial cutbacks that Sid came up with the final plan.

'Uric,' he said, 'why do we need a girl at all?'

'For you,' I replied.

'Well, I guess I can manage without one,' he said. 'If there are only the three of us, maybe we could tow a light trailer, a U-Haul if we can get one, what do you think?'

'It seems,' I replied, 'to be the only solution as we can't get a "back-up" but we will have to restrict our gear to bare essentials.'

'Like no *kreplach* soup,' he replied gloomily. I nodded somberly.

After wasting another day frantically 'phoning around London to try and hire a U-Haul trailer, we admitted defeat and called Beer. He said he knew of a local guy who would make one within a few days, just leave it to him. That problem taken care of, we dashed around from bank to bank collecting case loads of obscure currency in low denominations. Our final consultations and visa checks with the RAC were completed, we felt qualified for a rest period. Alas it was not to be, there were medical examinations, nasty multi-injections for every tropical disease from beriberi to the dreaded Nadgers' and a precise schedule for anti-malaria pills to be taken. Finally I squeezed in an hour to do my own shopping.

I stocked up with camera film and purchased a little Sony

short-wave radio and felt justified in buying myself something which I had always wanted, a genuine Swiss army knife with all the trimmings. Despite our jettisoning several pieces of equipment due to chronic lack of space we still had enough gear ready to kit out a small army of mercenaries. Sid, however, was still frantically scouring the local apothecaries for packets of vintage blue Gillette razor blades. He had assured me on several occasions that these rare items were well worth searching for and that he had used no other since being advised to do so by Mr Gillette whom he had met personally about half-a-century ago.

On the eve of departure Beer arrived driving our sparkling little MG towing its tiny trailer laden with spares and equipment. We then had to squeeze our own cases into the rig before battening it down and setting the alarm mechanism. In the nick of time we managed to contact Tony Mascarenhas, the elusive *Sunday Times* writer whose knowledge of India and Pakistan allowed us to fill in some vital gaps in our route. This was planned to take us through France, Germany, Austria, Hungary, Rumania, Bulgaria, Greece, Turkey, Iran, Afghanistan, Pakistan and on to the brand new Karakoram Highway over the top of the world into China.

Tony advised us, that despite all our written permissions from the highest sources we might just be a trifle optimistic about crossing the Karakoram Highway. Therefore he helped us to plan an alternative overland route crossing India to Madras, then by sea to Singapore, through Malaysia and Thailand, another sea voyage to Hong Kong and on to China.

September 1st, am – 'D-day' found us still rushing from bank to bank by taxi in an effort to untangle the mess of travellers cheques we had been lumbered with and which Sid had stuffed into his oversize briefcase.* Finally some sort of order emerged from the chaos and we arrived at the Portal gallery. There we were met by Harry Evans and a few friends and we all walked over to the Nuthouse for lunch. Beer remained, at his insistence, guarding the MG. Sid would obviously have preferred our departure lunch to have been at Blyumes and actually said on entering the Nuthouse that he hoped

---

* An article which like that of Passepartoute became an extension of his arm during the forthcoming months.

the food served therein would not portend the food we would be eating en route.

Actually any hardship that the health food caused him that day was negated somewhat by a conversation about his favourite artist George Grosz with Francis Bacon whom I had invited to join us.

Outside the gallery surrounded by well wishers and a lady traffic warden preparing to put a ticket on the waiting MG, we climbed aboard after lowering the canvas hood to facilitate *The Sunday Times* photographer, Bryan Wharton's shots. The fact that Bryan was required to accompany us as far as Paris and was expecting a lift with us was announced as we were just about to depart, and although painfully squashed into the overladen car we were all in a rumbustuous mood. As we started on our adventure Sid remarked to me driving along Bond Street:

'MG *mishegoyim.*'

Chapter 15

It is ironical that what should be the longest chapter in this book is in effect the shortest. My account of the Paris to Peking trip could easily fill another volume but from the outset it has not been my intention nor is it in my future plans to relate the saga in any detail. My memories are vivid and do include several amusing episodes which occurred during the early stages. Circumstances, however, including the temporary closure of *The Sunday Times* due to strike action created chronic difficulties for us en route.

It must be obvious to observers of human nature that a couple of curmudgeons like Sid and I placed in a cocktail shaker with a normally reserved English gentleman as the third ingredient would create a bitter potion when shaken for too long. Sid was in his mid-seventies and although remarkably fit for his age, a trip under such trying circumstances took its toll. We spent weeks without decent food and sleeping accommodation, due to a series of earthquakes, floods and political coups, where most of the time we were unable to make contact with the outside world. Thankfully the game little MG ran like a clock for the entire trip and despite our setbacks we did arrive home safely albeit in poor shape. Our objective to drive the car to Peking was almost achieved, we did get our wheels on the border of China. It was bureaucracy and not lack of courage that beat us.

The tragedy that this trip created was the irreparable rift it caused between Sid and myself. The last time I saw him was in our suite at the Penninsula Hotel in Hong Kong.*

However, one evening, about five months later, I picked up the 'phone in my London flat and was surprised to hear Sid's voice calling from New York. He simply asked me to help

---

* He eventually reached Peking by air but was immediately stricken with bronchial pneumonia, hospitalized and returned to Hong Kong as soon as he was able.

expedite the shipping of the MG (then back in England) to New York as I had agreed to do before the trip. Still, I was pleased he had called.

In retrospect, I think of that call as the completion of a wonderous circle that began with a discussion about an MG and ended the same way.

On the morning of October 18th, 1979, I heard on a radio news report that during the night S. J. Perelman had died peacefully in his sleep at the Gramercy Park Hotel, New York.

I was deeply grieved . . . I still am.

—————— Glossary ——————
of Yiddish Words

Shortly before completing this volume I was participating in one of my Sunday morning pleasures. That of listening to the evergreen BBC radio programme, *Letter from America,* written and narrated by Alistair Cook. He began his talk this week by telling us an episode of his social life. He and his wife had recently spent an enjoyable evening with friends at their New York apartment. His hosts that evening, like most of his New York friends, were Jewish.

Although close on fifty per cent of the New York population are Jewish I feel it goes well beyond that. The American Black people, Italians, and some other ethnic groups are almost as 'Jewish'. The lifestyle, language, food and above all humour of the Jews, is New York. Likewise the Jews themselves have assimilated Black and Italian culture and speech patterns, which makes New York such a wonderful, warm mixture of ideas. The Yiddish and Yinglish* which has become an integral part of the New York dialect is not, however, readily understood in London. We do, of course, have a Jewish population but only a fraction of New York's, and because of the size of London the Jewish sections are spread out and are sparse compared with New York's. Perhaps the closest we came to language integration was during the first third of this century when the London East End Jewish ghettoes existed, and the local Cockney population added some Yiddish words to their vocabulary. In London the influence was mostly reversed with the Jewish residents picking up the cockney lingo.

Today a few Yiddish words are beginning to be used more widely in London and some other large British cities, although rarely understood properly or pronounced correctly, they are

---

* A mixture of Yiddish and English.

infiltrating into our slang. The obvious reason for them becoming acceptable is that American TV programmes are now widely viewed in this country. The films of Woody Allen, Mel Brooks, Walter Matthau, George Burns, Phil Silvers etc. are popular but only partially understood by the average British audience. In the field of literature S. J. Perelman was known as a cult writer and appreciated by a small group of fanatics. But a few more recent American authors have been successful with Jewish themes; Philip Roth and Mordecia Richler* come to mind. For readers who wish to improve their Yiddish vocabulary I warmly recommend Leo Rosten's *The Joys of Yiddish*, available in Britain and USA.

Most Yiddish words have no exact English spelling, or even translation, they are phonetic guesswork, therefore if your own spelling of one of the words below is different from mine it means that our grandparents originated from a different *schtetl . . .†*

Barmitzvah If you don't know this one go to the bottom of the class, it's almost universal. It is the initiation ceremony that a thirteen-year-old Jewish boy has to endure in a synagogue before being accepted as a man.

Borscht Delicious beetroot soup, traditionally slurped by Jewish, Russian and Polish families.

Chasidic An ultra-religious Jew who follows the party line and wears the kind of gear you see in Woody Allen movies.

Chutzpah An act of intense effrontery which is tough to define. A kind of super cheek which leaves the recipient gasping in admiration at the sheer nerve of the perpetrator who always seems to get away with it.

Gelt Money, spondulicks, dough, bread, lolley, readies, rhino, mazuma, ackers, lucre, shekels. OK you got my meaning?

Haimisch(er) No relation to the Scottish gent with the bagpipes. A very important Jewish attribute it means warm,

---

* Canadian
† Work that one out for yourself.

genuinely friendly, informal, like family, on the same wavelength, understanding, no bullshit.

Kneidlach Lovely lumps of *matzoh* meal served with Jewish penicillin (chicken soup). The Chinese call them 'dim sum', the Irish 'dumplings'.

Kosher Well, if you haven't heard of kosher you must be a retarded Aborigine. Anyhow, just in case you are, it means food that has passed all the stringent Jewish dietary laws and can be eaten by the most orthodox. However, it has become a slang word for OK, legitimate, honest, etc.

Kreplach Another yum-yum dumpling, this time filled with meat or cheese and served in steaming hot soup.

Latkes Potato pancakes with guts, like chicken soup every Jewish Mother's speciality. Make a greasy mess on linen tablecloths and are lethal to the digestive system.

Matzoh A Jewish unleavened bread, especially formulated for passover but eaten throughout the year by aficionados, weight watchers, and those that just love the taste with chopped liver or blackcurrant jam, obtainable at almost any supermarket.

Mazel Good luck, to congratulate a Jewish person say '*Mazeltov*'.

Meshugge Means nuts, crazy, round the bend, looney or daft but in the nicest possible way.

Mishegaas Another version of 'Meshugge' but more of an activity or a craze which usually lasts for a brief spell. Like skateboards, walkmans or ginseng.

Mishegoyim The people who collectively take part in these potty activities.

Mitzeah Is what most Jews spend half their lives searching for. It's not quite the same as an ordinary bargain, it's better.

Rabbi Actually 'Rebbe' and it simply means teacher, a man of learning and wisdom. Not quite the same as a priest, parson, or other spiritual leader, although often regarded so in most Western societies.

Schlepp To lug parcels or heavy articles, walk or travel a long way on a fool's errand.

Schlock Like the decor in most Indian restaurants or Russian-made trousers.

Schloff A catnap, forty winks, a snooze in the armchair after a heavy lunch, and before returning to work at the factory.

Schmie To look around shops without buying anything, but not necessarily without any gelt.

Schmooze A comfortable, friendly chat with *haimischer* folk.

Schtetl The village or home town of the Ashkenazim or Eastern European Jew like from *Fiddler on the Roof,* or my own flop hit song from the abortive musical *Love in Blooms,* entitled *Ruebin and his kettle from the Schtetl.*

Schtuck Plain trouble. 'In *schtuck*' is often used by acquaintances of Jewish bankrupts to explain their predicaments to others.

Yarmulkah The little skullcap that religious male Jews wear at all times just as Sikhs wear a turban. It is customary during grace at Jewish wedding feasts for the not so religious male guests to be issued with *yarmulkahs* made of black tissue paper. These are so lightweight that should the guest be seated near the air conditioning, an electric fan, or in a draught the *yarmulkah* tends to leave the head and float off into space like a flying saucer.

Yiches Prestige, especially in the eyes of the community. Nothing to do with owning two Rolls Royces.

Yiddish The language used and devised by East European Jews. Containing a delightful and amusing hotch-potch of German, Russian, Polish, Ukranian, and English, which, when coupled with the exact hand gestures, shoulder-shrugs and head movements, becomes almost universally self-explanatory. It is what Esperanto should have been but is not.